am i that man?

How Heroes, Role Models and Mentors Can Shape Your Life

Edited by Brian R. Willis

am I that man?
How Heroes, Role Models and Mentors Can
Shape Your Life
Edited by Brian R. Willis

Copyright ©2013 by Brian R. Willis

ISBN: 978-0-9808819-5-0

Published by Warrior Spirit Books
A Division of Winning Mind Training Inc.
246 Stewart Green S.W., Suite #2486
Calgary, Alberta T3H 3C8, Canada

Visit our website at www.warriorspiritbooks.com

Cover By Cody Willis

Table of Contents

Foreword

Am I that man?

"The true measure of a man is not where he stands at times of comfort and convenience but rather where he stands at times of challenge and controversy." Those words were spoken by Dr. Martin Luther King Jr. many years ago and they can be heard over and over in the book you are about to read.

A few years back I learned a Formula for Development from retired U.S. Army Colonel Joseph LeBoeuf who currently is a Duke University professor.

Experiences + Intellectual Readiness + Reflection = Growth / Development.

Let's break it down:

We all have Experiences and when others share them with us, we learn those life lessons without having to go through them ourselves. At times experiences are when we take the final exam before we learn the lesson, yet those hard-knock lessons may be the ones we remember the most.

Intellectual Readiness is the academic approach to understanding a particular subject. I went Old School like Rodney Dangerfield (for the young folks--like Will Ferrell). At 56 years of age, I attended St. Mary's College of California for a Masters in Leadership. I learned about leadership across the dining room table from my Mom and Dad. I was truly raised by a village with my grandparents, aunts and uncles leading the way. I saw leadership when I played high school and college sports, when I joined the state police, and when I infiltrated the Mob--you can learn from negative as well as positive. I experienced leadership running the floors of the National Basketball Association for 25 years as a referee. I wanted to learn and study leadership theories and expand my intellectual readiness on the subject of leadership.

Reflection is the most difficult part of the formula because it calls on our ability to be introspective. Take time to reflect on what you have been exposed to and figure out how it will allow you to influence your personal, professional and world view growth.

It has been said that Personal Transformation takes place in a learning community because of the safe environment for growth in that setting.

am I that man? will take you on the journey described in the Growth/Development formula and provide that safe place for Personal Transformation.

Brian Willis and Ron Scheidt have given us all a growth opportunity with *am I that man?*

Some people GO through experiences while others GROW through experiences.

Enjoy the journey!

Bob Delaney

New Jersey State Police (ret.), NBA Referee (ret.), currently NBA Cares Ambassador and consultant.

Author of *COVERT, My Years Infiltrating the Mob* (USAToday best book of the year listing) and *Surviving the Shadows...A Journey of Hope into Post Traumatic Stress.*

Introduction

Imagine it is the end of your life and you find yourself standing on the balcony of a large church looking out over a sea of people with whom you have interacted throughout your life. They are all there to speak openly and honestly about you. They are your family, your friends, your coworkers, your bosses, people you coached, people you supervised, people who were role models and mentors to you. What do you want them to say about you? How do you want to be remembered when you die? More importantly, how do you want to be remembered for how you lived?

When Ron Scheidt first approached me about a book around the theme of the question "Am I that man?" I was both excited and nervous. As a father, husband, and trainer I was excited about the prospect of putting together a book that could provide tools, tactics and strategies for the young men in our society as they became fathers, husbands, coaches, trainers and leaders.

The prospect of writing for the book and the possibilities of seminars and training events based on this powerful question, however, were going to need some self-reflection. Transparency and honest self-reflection tends to make all of us nervous. Nerves are okay as long as you embrace them and do the work.

As the book moved forward, I had to continually ask myself two questions:

1. Am I that man (father, son, brother, husband, friend, coach, mentor, leader)?

2. What's Important Now? This question, which I refer to as Life's Most Powerful Question, always leads me back to the question Am I That…?

The answer to the first question was and still is "no." That bothered me for a while until I realized the question is in the present tense. The question is not about perfection; the question is about striving to be the best man you can be while still accepting you are human. To accept you are human requires accepting you are not perfect;

you have faults, you make mistakes, you make poor decisions, you say things that are hurtful to others, and you sometimes act in selfish ways.

The question "Am I that man?" is not about striving to be perfect, it is about striving to always be better tomorrow than you are today. It is about being human, learning from your mistakes and then moving forward a better man as a result of the experience.

This book is about role models, mentors and heroes. It is about the people who helped shape your life. It is about the lives you have shaped and influenced, and the lives you will shape and influence as you live out the many roles in your life. It is about self-reflection and self-evaluation. It is about learning from experience. It is about the continual course corrections you need to make to ensure you stay on the path through life that is true to that man you want to be for yourself. It is about being true to you. If you are true to yourself, you will be the man others in your life need you to be, and deserve you to be.

This book is not designed or intended for you to read and then pass along to a friend. This book is intended for you to make your own. You are encouraged to write your name in the front of it, dog-ear the pages, underline things that strike you as important and make notes in the margins. When you get to the end of each submission there is a page for you to make notes about your "Ah ha!" moments, your personal takeaways and at least one action item. You can then transfer the action item onto your calendar, Smartphone, tablet, day planner or whatever source you use to keep track of things you have committed to do. **The key is to take action**. You are encouraged to share information about the book with your friends, but make this book your own. Keep it someplace safe, keep it handy and keep going back to the book to review the key passages, thoughts and insights.

Take your time with this book. Read a chapter. Reflect on it. Use and process that which is useful to you right now, and set the other thoughts, ideas and strategies aside for now. They will likely become useful at some point in the future. Read another chapter and repeat

the process. The chapters can be read randomly or in sequence. With the exception of the submission that started all of this—"*Am I That Man?*" by Ron Scheidt—the rest of the submissions are not in order of significance or impact. Every essay is of significance and will have a different impact on you.

This is not a self-help book, this is a guidebook. Use it as your personal guide to be That Man.

Brian Willis

Am I That Man?

By Ron Scheidt

After almost twenty years as a United States Probation Officer, I can still hear the ringing phone that started it all. On the other end of the line was Burt Matthies, then—Chief U.S. Probation Officer of the District of Nebraska, asking if I would accept a position with his office. It was a proud moment and resulted in a decision that would change my life forever.

As I entered the twentieth and final year as a Senior U.S. Probation Officer—a career that was filled with tremendous satisfaction, numerous opportunities, and many wonderful memories—I found myself in a time of reflection. The thing I would miss the most was the relationships. I continued to reflect not only on career and work relationships but also on those early and intentional relationships that helped define and mold my very character.

I didn't know then, but two of the most influential people in my life—my mentors and role models—had begun preparing me long before that phone call in 1991. They were the ones who put me in a position to pursue a career with the United States Government and they were the ones that never let me forget where I came from. They taught me hard work, respect, integrity, values, and selflessness. Their investment profoundly influenced my life direction.

My brother, Roger "Bud" Scheidt, was my role model and mentor long before I even knew what those words meant. Although my mom did the best that she could, I grew up in a very dysfunctional family. My dad was a hard worker but an even harder drinker, and weekends were something to dread. My earliest memories of Bud were of him and his wife, Carolyn, picking me up as a young child and taking me to ball games, movies, out to eat—anything to get me out of that environment. He was not only a brother but also a father figure and a best friend. His selflessness was my salvation. I revered him as a man; even though he was my brother, he was everything my dad should have been but wasn't.

In my early adulthood, I had the opportunity to work in a steel plant alongside my brother, who was the production superintendent at the facility. While in this position, I continued to witness countless acts of his selfless behavior. On many days I can recall him commenting how much he was looking forward to the home-cooked lunch Carolyn had packed for him. Yet, it seemed that more often than not, he ended up giving this food away to an employee who didn't have the means to bring his own lunch that day. More importantly, he always did it in such a way that allowed the employee to maintain their pride and integrity. There are too many examples of his selflessness to recount; however the underlying theme was clear: he consistently placed the needs of others, including mine, before his own. He gave his time, talents, and treasures freely and without reservation.

In June 1985, my brother was diagnosed with pancreatic cancer and given less than a year to live. I'll never forget a car ride that he and I took the night he realized that the treatments weren't working. The doctors had said there was nothing more they could do and he needed to prepare for the end. Through the tears, I looked at the man who had been my stability and salvation and asked, as I had so many times before, "What are we going to do?" And for the first time in my life, the man who always had the answers said, "There's nothing we can do. But I'm not going to let something this small get me down." At his funeral six months later, as I stood next to my mom and Bud's family to follow the recessional, I felt the eyes of all 800 attendees on me and I asked myself, "Am I that man?"

The second major influence in my life was Bill Hunsaker, my junior high PE teacher and basketball coach. Following my dad's death, shortly after my thirteenth birthday, Coach seemed to innately understand my need for direction as a young male. At this pivotal point in my life, he intentionally invested in my development as an athlete and a young man. He provided encouragement, support and stability—I wanted to be just like him.

I had never in my wildest dreams imagined pursuing a college education, but Coach was able to see and encourage in me potential that I couldn't see in myself. It was only through this encouragement that I was able to fulfill my dream of teaching and coaching—like my idol.

Without his encouragement, my career in the field of criminal justice would have been unattainable. More than forty years later, Coach and I still talk several times a week, and I always seem to walk away with another life lesson. If you know Mayberry's Sheriff Andy Taylor, the television character, then you know Coach, too. He continues to be a role model and an inspiration to this day. I consider Coach to be among the biggest influences in my life and I often wonder, "Am I that man?"

Thinking of these two men and their tremendous influence on my life, I know their investment in me was intentional and their love was unconditional. I may not remember everything they ever said or did, but I will never forget how they made me feel. As I think of these two special men, I am always reminded of Bette Midler's famous rendition of "Wind Beneath My Wings."

It might have appeared to go unnoticed
But I've got it all here in my heart
I want you to know, I know the truth, of course I know it
I would be nothing without you

Did you ever know that you're my hero?
You're everything I wish I could be
I could fly higher than an eagle
For you are the wind beneath my wings

I encourage you to think about who these people are in your life. If you are fortunate enough to be blessed with a Bud or Coach already in your life, as I was, cherish and nurture that relationship. If not, I would encourage you to seek individuals actively and intentionally that will enhance your life and challenge your growth personally, professionally, and spiritually. I often wonder where I would be today if Bud and Coach hadn't invested in me and modeled in their own unique ways what it meant to be a man, a father, a husband, and a friend. Find that special person in your life. Those relationships—more than any career accomplishments—are what you will never forget.

Similarly I encourage you to intentionally seek opportunities to serve as a mentor and role model to others. You may never really know how profoundly your investment might impact someone. Maybe, just maybe, it will inspire them to positively alter the course of their life. Although Bud and Coach couldn't change the world, they certainly changed the world for one young man.

I encourage you to look outward and inward, and never stop asking yourself, "Am I that man?"

About the Author

Ron Scheidt, like all men, has experienced periods of struggle and uncertainty resulting in self-reflection. These reflections ultimately led him to develop a motivational presentation and write an article entitled *Am I that Man?* which appears in the book *If I Knew Then 2* (Brian Willis, Editor) and has served as the inspirational theme and title for the book *Am I That Man?*

Ron is challenged and proud to be the best father he can be to two adult sons (Evan and Martin) as well as the best husband and friend possible to his soul mate Jeri – all of whom have been the focus of many of the aforementioned reflections.

Professionally Ron is the Lead Natural Response Control Tactics Instructor with Community Corrections Institute and a retired Senior United States Probation Officer with the District of Nebraska. He has served as a faculty member of the Federal Judicial Center and as a National Defensive Tactics Instructor for the Office of Probation and Pretrial Services. He has trained and consulted for the Administrative Office of the United States Courts, Federal Judicial Center, American Probation and Parole Association and Federal Probation and Pretrial Officers Association.

He is a highly regarded guest speaker and instructor having presented on multiple topics at conferences and academies throughout the United States and Canada.

Ron can be contacted at Ron@amithatman.com

AM I THAT MAN

AH-HAHS:

TAKE AWAYS:

ACTION ITEM:

Who are your heroes? Why?
How have they influenced your life?

Your Life IS Your Legacy

By Brian Willis

Too often in today's world when asked about a legacy, people refer to the number of championships an athlete has won, the amount of financial wealth a person accumulated in their life, endowment funds or physical structures. Over the years, I have come to the realization that a legacy is something you create every day that you live, rather than something you leave behind when you die. Robert Louis Stevenson captured this philosophy when he said, "Do not judge each day by the harvest you reap, but by the seeds you plant."

When you think of a legacy as something you create every day you live, you begin to understand that in your life you live many roles. In my life those roles include son, father, husband, coach, mentor, brother, teacher, leader, and friend. For each of those roles I must continually ask myself Life's Most Powerful Question—What's Important Now? When I pause to ask that question, it leads me to two other powerful questions:

1. Am I that…?
2. What is my legacy as…?

Am I that son?

My parents (Bob and Terry) have been a tremendous influence in my life and have always been great role models. They are positive people who place family first in their lives. They are continually touching the lives of others through their generosity, friendship, acts of kindness and their genuine interest in other people. One of the greatest parenting gifts they gave me was their unconditional love. I have not always been a great son. I made some choices in my life that hurt them more than I will ever truly comprehend. Through it all they have loved and supported me. What is my legacy as a son? Am I the son they raised me to be? Am I the son my parents deserve me to be? Am I the son my parents need me to be as they get older?

Am I that father?

I am blessed with two amazing sons, Jesse and Cody. I am continually inspired by their creativity, their work ethic, their love of life and their wisdom. As adults they serve as a sounding board for me and continually offer advice, direction and clarity. As they were growing up I was a Cub leader and a football, basketball and soccer coach; I strove to be their biggest supporter and fan. At times I was a good dad and at times I struggled. Through it all they have loved and supported me and now they serve to inspire me. What is my legacy as a father? Am I the father Jesse and Cody need me to be? Am I the father Jesse and Cody deserve me to be?

Am I that husband?

At the time of this writing, my wife Lynda and I have been married for over thirty years. In that time she has put up with my shift work, my tendencies towards being a workaholic, my idiosyncrasies, my moods, and my flaws that others often do not see. Through it all she has been there to support me and love me unconditionally. What is my legacy as a husband? Am I the husband Lynda deserves to have? Am I the husband Lynda deserves me to be?

Am I that brother?

I have two brothers, Jim and Larry, and a sister, Sandra. Each one is very different, yet they are all amazing people and extremely successful in their lives. Benjamin Jowett said, "The real measure of our wealth is how much we'd be worth if we lost all our money." By that measure they are all wealthy people. They are people who have touched many lives, who value family and have shown me unconditional love and support. What is my legacy as a brother? Am I the brother my siblings deserve me to be? Am I the brother my siblings need me to be?

Am I that leader?

In the latter part of my law enforcement career and now in my career
as a trainer I have found myself in leadership positions. As I reflect
and learn I realize now how little I knew about leadership. I did the
best I could with the tools I had. Sometimes I did well, other times
I didn't. I have learned that leadership is never about rank, position
or title. Leadership is about action and interaction. I also now realize
that everyone in an organization is in a position to lead; the question
is whether you choose to lead. What is my legacy as a leader? Am I the
leader people expect me to be? Am I the leader people need me to be?

Am I that teacher?

Since 1989 I have had the pleasure, privilege, challenge,
responsibility and honor of being a trainer. For the first few years
I was a part-time trainer in addition to my other duties with the
police department. Since the summer of 1994 I have been a full-
time trainer. There is a saying, "When the student is ready the
teacher will appear." In order to be that teacher you have to be
ready for the student. You have to be on your game. You have to
be ready to give your best every day regardless of what is going on
in your life. What is my legacy as a teacher? Am I the teacher my
students deserve? Am I the teacher my students need me to be?

Am I that role model?

I believe you do not set out to be a role model. You strive to be
the best you can be. As a result of those efforts you become a role
model to some. Many of the people I admire are very reluctant to
accept the label of role model. They are humble people who do not
believe they are role models. The reality is that being a role model
is not something you choose. It is something that is chosen for you
by others who chose to model their behaviors and their lives after
you. It is important to understand and accept that you are a role
model for someone so live your life accordingly. What is my legacy
as a role model? Am I modeling a life to be proud of?

Am I that mentor?

A mentor is defined as a wise and trusted counselor or teacher. I like to think of the word more as a verb than a noun; something you do rather than something you are. Like role models in my life, many of those who have mentored me would refute that label. They do not see themselves as a mentor. I too am uncomfortable with that label. I believe we all got to where we are because other people helped us. They helped us by their willingness to listen, by sharing advice, by sharing their knowledge, by sharing their time, and by sharing their passion. They did not set out to 'mentor' me. They simply were willing to help me when I needed help. What is my legacy as a mentor? Am I willing to share my time and energy with others? Am I there for others when they need someone to help and guide them?

Am I that friend?

W. Clement Stone said, "Be careful the environment you choose for it will shape you; be careful the friends you choose for you will become like them." Who are your friends? Who are the people in your life you choose to spend the most time with? Are they positive, upbeat and supportive? Or are they the whining, sniveling malcontents and the energy vampires of the world? More importantly what kind of friend are you? Do you support your friend's dreams, hopes and desires? Or do you always find fault in them or their plan? Are you someone they can rely on even when things are bad and they have screwed up or are you a fair-weather friend? Is friendship a two-way street or are you focused on what's in it for you? What is my legacy as a friend? Am I a true friend who can always be relied on?

Am I willing to allow myself to be human?

Now this may sound strange, but this is not some far-out alien thing. I believe to be human means to accept you have faults and weaknesses. To be human means to accept you will make mistakes, and to focus on learning from those mistakes. To be human means you will fail, but failing to accomplish a task does not make you a failure. To be human means that you will not always be that father, husband, friend, brother, and teacher when people need you to be, but you always strive to be. To be human is to accept these faults and commit to always being better tomorrow than you are today. To be human is to pursue excellence, not perfection. To be human means you have the capacity to forgive, the capacity to forgive yourself, and the capacity to forgive others.

Regardless of what stage of your life you are in, I encourage you to take time to reflect and to ask yourself these three questions:

1. What's Important Now?
2. What is the legacy I am creating?
3. Am I that...?

About the Author

Brian Willis is the proud father of two amazing young men (Jesse and Cody) and is honored to have been married to his beautiful wife Lynda since June of 1981.

Brian is an internationally recognized thought leader, speaker, trainer, writer and President of the innovative training company Winning Mind Training (www.winningmindtraining.com).

Brian was a full time police officer with the Calgary Police Service from 1979 to 2004. He is the recipient of a Lifetime Achievement Award in recognition of his contribution and commitment to Officer Safety in Canada and was named Law Officer Trainer of the Year for 2011.

Brian serves as the Deputy Executive Director for the International Law Enforcement Educators and Trainers Association (ILEETA). He is the editor and contributing author for the acclaimed books *W.I.N.: Critical Issues in Training and Leading Warriors* and *W.I.N. 2: Insights Into Training and Leading Warriors*, *If I Knew Then: Life Lessons From Cops on the Street* and *If I Knew Then 2: Warrior Reflections*. He is also a contributing writer for the book *Warriors: On Living with Courage, Discipline and Honor.*

Brian Can be contacted at Brian@amithatman.com

Your Life IS Your Legacy

Ah-Hahs:

Take Aways:

Action Item:

An Ode to Failure

By Jesse Willis

> *"The brick walls are there for a reason. The brick walls are not there to keep us out; the brick walls are there to give us a chance to show how badly we want something. The brick walls are there to stop the people who don't want it badly enough."*
> —Randy Pausch, The Last Lecture

Often in our society, praise and adoration follow success. Icons and heroes are remembered for their great victories, glorious feats and grand accomplishments. When you delve deeper into the lives of those who influence us, however, you begin to realize that without exception these great successes were preceded by epic failures.

When I look at the men who've acted as mentors and influenced me most in my life, the theme of failure is a common one. I see high school dropouts and nights spent sleeping in cars and in parks. I see failed businesses and missed goals along with moments of weakness and tears. At the time, their flaws and faults may have earned these men criticism and ridicule, but in the end it earned them my respect.

Clearly these men didn't seek out failure, but it was the lessons wrenched from the claws of defeat that gave them the strength and conviction to become the leaders they are today. The truth is that you cannot achieve anything great in this life without failure. After all, without failure you can never experience the limits of your capabilities. Finding our true potential requires us to strain against our perceived capacities…to step to the edge of our limited beliefs, close our eyes and jump. To achieve meaningful growth requires us to accept our vulnerability and the imperfect nature of our humanity.

Failure is like a great teacher. Sometimes it lets us down gently, giving us a soft reminder that we've gone astray with a gentle nudge back onto the right path. And sometimes, usually when we need it the most, failure brings the ruler down hard onto the desk of our lives, smacks us across the head and tells us to wake up and get our act together.

The problem is that we're conditioned to view failure in a negative light. We've been taught to associate failure with weakness and shame. We're inundated with images of success without including the failures that prefaced those victories. We're shown sports highlight reels, but never in the context of the thousands of mistakes required to build an athlete's skill to that level. We see actors and actresses gracing the covers of magazines after an Oscar-worthy performance, but we never see the footage of the rejections and failed auditions from earlier in their career. We see the headlines as an entrepreneur sells his business to a major conglomerate for millions without being given the background on that same entrepreneur's previous bankruptcies and failed ventures.

I'm acutely aware of the role failure can play in creating success. Often people perceive my current physical condition without noticing the stretch marks left by the one hundred pounds I lost getting here. People praise me for my current success in business without commenting on the two failures that preceded it. They admire the confidence in my voice when addressing a group of students without hearing the shaky, choppy and frightened intonation that was the hallmark of my early public speaking engagements. I have only become the man I am today through the mistakes of my past, and I will only grow to be the man I aspire to be through the failures that lie ahead.

Although all of my mentors have experienced failure, it is not failure in and of itself that defines them. What defines these men is how they've dealt with the adversity they've encountered in their lives. In order to harness the wisdom of defeat we must embrace it. We must make friends with failure and welcome it with open arms. We must use failure as that yardstick that lets us know we've pushed ourselves to our limits. I now yearn for those moments when I can look in the mirror, feel the fear rise from the pit of my stomach and smile with the realization that the feeling of uncertainty is simply a compass pointing me towards my next challenge.

We can all recite one of the countless rags-to-riches, victory in spite of setback stories from history: whether it be Michael Jordan being cut from his varsity basketball team only to become one of the greatest athletes of all time, or the Spartans suffering defeat at the Battle of Thermopylae, all the while buying precious time for a final Greek victory over the Persians. The challenge I put forth to you is to evaluate those "failures" in your own life and to see them for what they are…feedback. After all, failure is simply life telling us there's a better way to achieve what we want. Defeat requires acceptance and is therefore a choice. We can either accept failure as final or we can choose to find another way to achieve our objective.

Let me be clear, I am not saying that you should seek out failure. Failure should never be your goal. No team steps on the field hoping to lose. No one applies for a job with the goal of being rejected. No one starts a business with the vision of going bankrupt. My point is that too often people let the fear of failure and rejection hold them back from following their passion and their dreams. I've watched too many amazing people squander their potential because they were immobilized by images of failure. My greatest fear in life is sitting on my deathbed and realizing that I held back, that I played it safe, that I missed the opportunity to live a life of meaning, significance and passion because I was scared of what might have been.

The inspiration I've taken from the mentors in my life has lead me to embrace the faults in my past and accept the failures that lie ahead of me. My vulnerability has become my greatest strength. I can honestly say that if today was my last day on earth, I would be completely content with the choices I've made to this point… as imperfect as they've been. I hope you can find the same level of contentment in your life.

I'll leave you with one of my favourite quotes from business mogul Mark Cuban: "It doesn't matter how many times you fail. It doesn't matter how many times you almost get it right. No one is going to know or care about your failures, and neither should you. All you have to do is learn from them and those around you because... All that matters in business is that you get it right once. Then everyone can tell you how lucky you are."

About the Author

Jesse is one of Western Canada's top young wine professionals and is the co-owner of Vine Arts Wine and Spirits, a specialty wine shop in Calgary, Alberta.

Jesse found his love for wine after a shoulder injury forced him to move away from his career as a fitness trainer and seek out a temporary position that only required the use of one arm. As luck would have it, hefting a glass of wine fit the bill and the rest is history. Jesse holds his Sommelier Diploma from the International Sommelier Guild and is also the wine director at Taste Restaurant in Calgary.

In addition to his love of wine, Jesse remains active in the fitness community, recently completing his Crossfit Level 1 Trainer certificate.

For more information on Jesse and Vine Arts please visit www.vinearts.ca

AN ODE TO FAILURE

AH-HAHS:

TAKE AWAYS:

ACTION ITEM:

List two important role models
in your life.
What impact have they had?

Dare to be Great!

By Bill Mikaluk

My father meant the world to me. He was truly a great man, and not just by my standards. Everyone loved him and it was apparent that he loved them, too. My dad was always very easy to be around. He made people feel like they were the most important and only person in the room. He would always give everyone his time and attention…and he always had time for us kids, no matter what he was doing. He lived a "back to basics" lifestyle and today, over twenty years after my father's passing, people still talk about him with praise and honour.

I remember the time when I told him I had applied to be a policeman. He simply said, "You'll get in." He always had confidence in me and he constantly encouraged me to be my best. The interesting thing was that he challenged me to *be* my best, not just *do* my best. For him, character development was far more significant than titles or possessions, or creating a masked personality to impress others. He may not have known the exact words, but he certainly lived the Bible verse, "A good name is more desirable than great riches." Because of his influence, I grew to believe that greatness comes from being sincere and genuinely selfless. This selflessness, over time, automatically transpires into greatness.

The concept of selflessness brings to mind another great experience I had when I was in the final semester of attaining my Bachelor of Education degree. Mr. Burak, my practicum teacher, noticed that I lacked the spark he was looking for in a new teacher. While working with him, I was to instruct a wrestling class several times a week, but I knew almost nothing about the sport. I was lost and he knew it. After several less-than-spectacular teaching sessions, he suggested that for one upcoming class I instruct "movement skills" related to wrestling, rather than wrestling itself, and use a teaching delivery method that I was more familiar with, such as gymnastics. Finally, as he further prepared me for success, he challenged me with the words, "Don't think about the teaching aspect, *think*

about the kids; and when you come in tomorrow, *dare to be great!*"
Wow…what did that mean? Dare to be great? Me? I just wanted to
teach these kids something they could use and hopefully provide
an opportunity for them to have fun in the process. Dare to be
great? Is that what my dad was talking about when he encouraged
me to *be* my best and not just *do* my best?

Challenged by Mr. Burak (and thoughts of my father's words),
I planned and delivered an outstanding wrestling/gymnastics
session! The kids were alive and on fire as I guided them through a
series of activities, movements and challenges. I demonstrated and
joined them in various strength, agility, flexibility and endurance
exercises. They loved it, and so did I…and it showed! What made
the difference? I knew it was because I chose to focus on the students
and not on myself or on my teaching. When Mr. Burak dared me
to be "great," I took that as an opportunity to consider the process
of *how* to teach, rather than the product of *what* to teach. I chose
to *be* great, not just *do* great as a teacher. It worked amazingly well
at the time, but I'm embarrassed to admit that unfortunately I still
didn't quite *get it* for the long term, and eventually I forgot the
lesson learned.

The morning of January 1, 1990 when the Lord took my father, I
knew from that moment forward life for me would be very different
—a large part of *me* was now missing. My brother and I were both
reminiscing (and hurting) when he looked at me and quietly said,
"Well Bill, we have very big shoes to fill." And that's when it hit me.
In that instant I finally got it. As I reflected on my father's life, I
finally understood what it truly meant to *be* great. It was a mind-
shift, a total change in perspective. I remembered all that my dad
had done for me and for us, and I finally understood what he meant
when he encouraged me to *be* great. He was telling me to consider
others before myself. He wanted me to keep other people first in my
life and demonstrated that greatness equals selfless living! He was
daring me to be great, just like Mr. Burak had.

I also now realize that this progression to greatness in life doesn't
happen overnight, but rather occurs in stages. I believe we go

through a progression of five stages—from "learning" something to eventually "leaving" something—and it's in the leaving stage that our greatness shines through in selfless living.

These five stages to greatness include 5 L's:

 »Learn it,

  »Live it,

   »Love it,

    »Lead it,

     »Leave it!

Stage 1: Learn it (*my mind*):

I first need to understand something before I can apply it effectively in my life. For example, I need to learn the rules of the game of soccer, as well as the key concepts of coaching, before I can be an effective soccer coach.

Stage 2: Live it (*my body*):

Once I know something, I can put it into practice and do it. Continuing with the soccer coach example, I must practice the skills and techniques, both of soccer and of coaching, in order to utilize these effectively in the weekly practices.

Stage 3: Love it (*my heart*):

The next progression is to do something *repeatedly* until it becomes a part of my character and my very being. When I truly enjoy what I'm doing, my attitude shifts and becomes infectious to others. Now that I know what to do and how to do it, I must ensure that the kids playing soccer perceive me as truly enjoying being their coach. I can also now make "fun" a part of every practice for both myself and the players. Not because I have to, but because I really enjoy coaching and I want the players to realize that soccer is about far more than just improving individual soccer skills and winning games. It's also about personal development and growth.

Stage 4: Lead it (*my spirit*):

In this stage, the "doing" turns into "being." I *become* the person/ coach that I've been practicing to be, and also now share this with others through specific mentoring and coaching strategies. For example, my soccer practices become more structured around not only skill enhancement and various strategies and plays, but also include teamwork, leadership and personal growth portions... encouraging the kids (by example) to also coach themselves and each other.

Stage 5: Leave it (*my legacy*):

This is the stage where true greatness occurs! My character (*the real me*) has finally aligned with my personality (the *me* that others see). This is when my success becomes significance, and my passion turns into purpose! For me it isn't enough to be a great coach only on the field. I want to make sure that when my players (and my spouse, children, friends, etc.) see me outside of the coaching field, they see my consistent character as someone truly interested in them as individuals.

As I reflect further on what it means to be great, I often ask myself: What impact am I having on those around me? How will my wife, kids, family and friends remember me? What's my legacy? How will I pass the baton? Both my father and Mr. Burak were selfless. They lived and shared their values and priorities. They left their legacy. They became heroes to me and to others. Will I also be a hero to someone?

As a teacher, policeman and coach—and more importantly as a husband, father, and friend—I continually strive to be more selfless every day...and perhaps someday, hopefully, even be considered "great." My father was great. Mr. Burak was great. To their benefit, they both encouraged me, no *dared* me, to also be great. I'm up for that challenge! I truly *want* to be great...not for my own glory, but for *others'* sake.

It comes down to this: I think greatness is found in the everyday...

me being *me*, and living a life that I'm proud of, more selfless and less selfish. As I align my personality with my character and live by my core values, I dare myself every day to become great, and I look forward to leaving my legacy of greatness...of simply being *me*, my best me! How about you? Are you working toward greater selflessness? Do your character and personality align? Are you "*you*" every day...without the mask? Have you made the decision to *learn it, live it, love it, lead it* and *leave it* each day? Will you dare to be selfless? Will you dare to make a difference? Will you dare to be someone's hero? Will you *dare to be great*?

About the Author

Bill Mikaluk is a Christian, a husband and a father of two children. He is an eighteen-year veteran police instructor with the Edmonton Police Service. He is also a teacher and a certified professional coach. Bill can be contacted at bmikaluk@gmail.com or REALifeSuccess@gmail.com.

DARE TO BE GREAT!

AH-HAHS:

TAKE AWAYS:

ACTION ITEM:

He Didn't Tell Me How to Live

By Scott Westerman

> *He didn't tell me how to live; he lived, and let me watch him do it.*
> —Clarence Budington Kelland

My son had his first solo evening with his three-week-old on Friday night. While Mom was enjoying her first post-pregnancy night out with the girls, Brandon and Hudson held the fort. When he called to tell me about it, Brandon said, "I never knew I could love someone this much."

I'm sure he could hear the smile in my voice when I answered, "Now you can fully understand exactly how I feel about you."

For better or worse, the man he has become has a lot to do with what he learned from me. I'm far from perfect, and I've made more than my share of parental mistakes. Whatever success I may have had is due to the role models who helped me become the man I am today.

My father, "The Real Scott Westerman," is one of the best. Through the example of his own life, he gave me eleven insights that I've tried to embed in my DNA. They were the gifts his father passed on to him.

Make a difference for all the world—Dad's father, W. Scott Westerman Sr., was a distinguished music major at the University of Michigan, turned Methodist Missionary, turned beloved Ohio pastor, turned electronics enthusiast. I have a box of his sermons in my closet, each one succeeding in translating the often-confusing chapter and verse into meaningful messages that inspired his parishioners to model the Golden Rule. My father guided the Ann Arbor Public Schools through the turbulent sixties with courage and grace. He went on to be the Dean of Education at Eastern Michigan University, influencing a generation of educators while building the finest teacher education program in the nation.

Give your all—Both Dad and I have comforting memories of seeing the reflections of the car lights dancing across our bedroom walls late in the evening when our respective fathers came home. They attacked every day with enthusiasm, every project with near total commitment and filled every waking hour with a giving soul.

Seek balance—Dad believes that it was the workload and not Grandpa's milieu of childhood health issues that brought on his first heart attack, at age 45. Now in his 80s, my father still lives on his own, exercises every other day and continues to say, "I love my life!" He credits his health and exuberance to a continued life of learning, friendship and service.

Be inclusive—Both my father, and my own personal commitment to diversity, have roots in Grandpa's courageous integration of the church Boy Scout troop—long before it was the common thing to do. And Grandpa and Grandma had a habit of adopting church members with disabilities, going the extra mile to help each get the most out of life. Sometimes the most challenging thing about being a dad is finding the love when your kids need it most.

Develop diverse interests—Grandpa's passion was his music, but he also excelled in basketball, track, gymnastics, swimming and boxing. He was a fisherman, a bird watcher, a gardener and dog lover. Late in life, he developed an interest in electronics; building antennas for his shortwave receiver and recording television and radio programming for soldiers serving in Viet Nam. He passed that eclecticism along to his son. Dad tells me that the only stressor in his life today is his struggle with finding time to do everything he wants to do.

Have faith—Grandpa's was a Christian life, but like the Dali Lama, my own father would encourage you to seek your own spiritual path. Faith, whether it be in deity or the ordered mysteries of science, is at once alluring and baffling, exciting and frustrating. I learned from my male mentors that if you build your own foundation of faith it can keep you grounded through the strongest hurricanes, the harshest spotlight and the darkest night.

Be well read—Being up on current events and the latest literature was part of all our lives growing up. The things we discovered in newspapers and between the covers of good books danced through our minds, leaving notions that often sprouted like seeds into new and even more powerful ideas.

Get an education and seek to become a better person—Most of us are but a generation or two away from a time when college was the exception to the rule. In our parents' and grandparents' time, education meant drinking knowledge with a desert thirst, trying to fully understand and sometimes challenge what we were taught. Good grades were a goal but were secondary to the desire for real comprehension. Those learning skills served our forefathers well as we recovered from the Great Depression, fought a World War and learned to make sense of things like the Iron Curtain. Having the courage to face any personal demons you may have will also teach your children that we are all imperfect. It's ok to recognize it, and to show by your own example that life's too short not to get help while you enjoy the ride.

Don't do it all yourself—Both my grandfather and my dad were the first ones to admit that they could not have been effective parents without support. In our home, my mom was well prepared and totally dedicated to providing that assistance. But it went well beyond their union. They made sure that the right teachers appeared when we needed them. They exposed us to a diverse array of individual lifestyles (mostly good and a few bad) and had the courage to ultimately let us make our own choices. They empowered and supported our teachers to correct our self-defeating behaviors soon after they occurred, nearly always in private unless a public lesson was a teachable moment.

Be joyful—Whenever I would call Grandpa on the phone during my youth, he was always glad to hear from me. He was fascinated by new ideas. Even as the years slowed him down, he was always able to find a mother lode of silver linings surrounding every cloud. My own children report the same phenomenon when they call my dad.

Be present and be who you are—My father harbors a not-so-secret regret. He attacked the other things on this list with such intensity that he feels he was not present enough in our lives. I disagree. There was never a key question I had that he didn't patiently answer. There was never a major event in my life that he didn't attend, and whenever and wherever he was, he always responded to my phone calls. In those times of rebellion that inevitably touch each generation, he was patient when he needed to be, firm when he had to be and was always true to his beliefs, even when they were not popular.

I haven't always lived up to these ideals, but I've tried to live by them. I strive every day to be able to point to my father and honestly say, "I am that man." I hope that Brandon has integrated the good things he may have learned from the men in his family into his outlook. The best legacy I can wish for is the day he might take his son's hand, point to me and say, "I am that man."

What if you have not been lucky enough to land in a family with a strong father figure? Look about you. Dad's ideals live in many men and women that you may know. They are the essence of our most inspiring leaders. If you don't have a good biological role model, create your own. We are in fact the sum total of our genetics, our experiences, and most importantly, what we have learned from these experiences. We become who we associate with, so surround yourself with positive examples of extraordinary human beings. Forgive those who hurt you and forgive yourself for your own inevitable mistakes.

And be thankful. When someone has made a difference in your life, tell them. Even the most self-actualized has self-doubts. And we all long to love and be loved. Don't be so concerned about political correctness that you're afraid to hug those you love with intensity and often.

Seeking to understand, to pursue worthy dreams, to find something to appreciate in every human being, and modeling productive behaviors for the next generation; these are the keys to strong families, long-term success in every endeavor, and perhaps even world peace.

What would the world be like if each of us tried doing this every single day?

These are times when good male role models are in short supply.

Why not be one? If you do, then someday, someone else will point to you and say,

"I am that man."

About the Author

Scott Westerman is the Associate Vice President for Alumni Relations and Executive Director of the Michigan State University Alumni Association. During his career, he has been a broadcaster, aviator, martial arts instructor, entrepreneur and cable TV executive. His interests range from writing computer software to skydiving with the US Army Golden Knights. Scott's bestselling book, *The Spartan Life*, is a collection of essays on leadership and he lectures widely on "making passion your personal brand." During his college days at MSU he was a regular midnight ride-along with his warrior friends at the East Lansing Police Department.

HE DIDN'T TELL ME HOW TO LIVE

AH-HAHS:

TAKE AWAYS:

ACTION ITEM:

Tougher than Woodpecker Lips

By Chuck Soltys

If you look back at your life, most would say they had at least one individual who was there for them, someone who significantly impacted their life in a positive way. My individual is, without question, my father. He is the most significant mentor and role model in my life.

My father's family was hit hard by tough economic times, so he made the decision to drop out of high school and get a job to help feed the family. The war in Korea broke out and he enlisted in the Air Force as soon as he was old enough. While in the military, he earned his G.E.D. He then married my mother and they had four children in four years. He worked several jobs to keep food on our table, but never lost sight of the importance of an education and enrolled in college classes at night. As the youngest of four children, I was eighteen years old when my father earned his Bachelor's Degree. I saw my dad walk across the stage to receive his diploma. It was a proud moment in Soltys' family history.

My father's messages were simple. He would tell me, "Son, I'm not here to be your friend, I'm here to give you direction in life. You are not going to like all my decisions and you certainly aren't going to agree with most of them at the time, but if I guide you in the right direction we'll be friends. You'll see." He really only wanted one thing for his kids; he wanted to give us better opportunities than he had. He taught me the value of hard work and that life is merely a series of choices, good ones and bad ones, and both had consequences that could change my life. He taught me that honesty and integrity meant something and that your word and a handshake were the only contract needed. And he taught me to dream big, to believe in myself, and above all that my name meant something, not just to me but to everyone in my family. Never dishonor it. And that message applied when I wore a uniform as well. Anything I did, positive or negative in uniform or out, would reflect on everyone who wore that uniform, much like my family name.

When we were kids, my dad bought my brother and me each a pair of real leather boxing gloves. This was his way of letting us settle our own scores and blow off some steam. My brother was four years older than me, and this was his license to beat the crap out of me. In my brother's mind the bouts were sanctioned by virtue of the man who provided the gloves. I knew that if I wanted to ease the beatings at all, I would have to get tougher quickly...and I did.

When I disagreed with my father on his decisions and flared my chest a bit, he would look at me and say, "Son, anytime you think you're tough enough, we'll go downstairs and put the gloves on." Even as I grew considerably taller than my dad and outweighed him by almost 100 pounds, there was never a day that I thought I could take him. When I was young, it was the fear of a severe butt-whooping. When I got older, it was the profound respect I had for him. My father was tough but fair. He may have been small in stature, but he was tougher than woodpecker lips.

My dad grew up in a tough neighborhood on the Southside of Chicago where hard work, often shift work, lead many to hard drinking afterwards. Exhausting physical labor, tough street ethos, and the stress of making ends meet were a volatile concoction. Beating your wife and even your kids was a normal occurrence at the end of the day for some. Not for my dad. He had it as tough as anyone in the neighborhood, but he wasn't a heavy drinker and he never raised a hand to my mother. He worshipped her and still does. He showed us by example that it was cool to treat women with dignity and respect. One way to set my dad off was to upset my mom. If you did that, you were sure to get your cage rattled. He would always tell us, "Your mom was here before you guys, and she will be here after you've grown and moved out. So if you want to know where my loyalty rides, there you have it."

My father knew he could not be with us at all times. So he did his best to set a good example and to lay a solid foundation for good decision making. He made sure we chose our company wisely. "Surround yourself with winners," he would say. "If you're the smartest person in the room, you're in the wrong room. The world is full of people who will work twice as hard to pull you down to their level than they will to try to come up to yours. Don't waste a moment of your life on people like that."

In my last year of high school, I got a little too big for my britches and felt I knew how to run the football team better than the new head coach. In a heated moment, I did something I had never done before…I quit.

I hadn't yet realized that the last thing a coach, or any authority figure for that matter, wanted to hear was a cocky seventeen-year-old who thought he knew it all.

It wasn't often that my father stepped in on everyday events in my life, but he knew how impulsive and out of character this was. He saw my heartbreak and, without my knowledge, he called the coach and asked if he would consider taking me back on the team. The coach told my father that he never told me to quit and that I could come back anytime I wanted, but that I shouldn't expect to waltz back in and take a starting spot.

My father sat me down and told me about the conversation he had with the coach. He explained that this was a defining moment in my life and that we all make mistakes. It's how we respond to those mistakes that ultimately determine success or failure. He told me I could go back to the team, but it wouldn't be easy. I would have to work twice as hard if I had any chance of earning back the respect of the coaches and my teammates. My closest friends were part of that team and they didn't take my actions lightly.

My father asked me how I intended to handle this. Was I going to be the guy ten years down the road, sitting on the bar stool at the local tavern complaining about how I was wronged in life? Or was I going to swallow my pride and go back, fix what was broken and see what I could salvage?

My father was right. It wasn't easy going back. It was a struggle for the remainder of the season. My hasty decision that year left me few options for college. The only option, other than to end up as that guy on the bar stool, was to go to a local community college and start fresh. I went there, worked hard and kept my mouth shut. I went on to have two exceptional football seasons at the community college. My second season I was named captain of the team and received conference, state, and national honors, which lead to some offers to play football at the university level.

As I look back on my decision to play Division 1 football, there is no question it was a lofty goal. It was the proverbial "jump into the deep end of the pool to see if you can swim." This was the first time all of my father's messages began resonating at the same time. I had dreamed big, I believed in myself, I worked hard, and champions surrounded me. I had earned the privilege of wearing a uniform steeped in tradition and rich in history, and it had my family name in bold print on the back. I would not achieve the accolades at this level as I did at the community college, but few do. I may have faired better at a smaller school but then again, you play to your competition, and if I had it to do again, I would choose the same path. One thing is certain; I shared that gridiron with some of the best to ever play the game.

I had a wonderful experience in college; I made lifelong friends and laid the foundation for a successful career. Graduation day was emotional because I knew things would never be the same. Now it was time to go out and find a job. My dad asked me where I was going to graduate school. I said, "Dad, I've had it with school. I don't care if I open another book in my life." He said, "Son, if you think your learning stops with this diploma, you're sadly mistaken. It's just the beginning. Do you remember the guy who was asleep in his books at the kitchen table every morning when you were getting ready for school? Don't do it the way I did. Get your Master's or law degree. This is as easy as it's going to get."

Looking back a quarter of a century, I'm glad I stayed in school and completed my Bachelor's degree. I only wish I had listened to my dad and gone to graduate school back then. Once again, he was right…life does happen. For a guy who at times I thought didn't know much, he sure seemed to be spot on most of the time.

My father is now in his eighties. He has beaten cancer twice and is currently battling a litany of health issues that come with age. Throughout my life, my dad has given me guidance and advice, both directly and indirectly. This advice not only paved my path to success but also provided the road map for choosing the right path over the wrong one. He is a sagacious man who was my GPS to maturity. The greatest thing he ever said to me was, "Son, I'm proud of you."

I have lived a charmed life. I have a wonderful wife and family, and materially I have it better than my dad ever did--nicer cars, a bigger house, a successful career, and much more. But I owe all that to him and to what he taught me by word and example. He is my hero, role model, mentor, and yes…my friend.

I believe our greatest mark of success is the values we impart to our children. If so, I may manage to equal my dad's success, but I will never be able to exceed it.

When people tell me I look like my father, I thank them, for that is a great compliment. When they tell me I act like my father, that is the greatest compliment anyone could ever give.

As Tina Wiens wrote in her hit song sung by Paul Overstreet, "Seein' My Father in Me":

I'm seein' my father in me

I guess that's how it's meant to be

And I find I'm more and more like him each day

At the risk of sounding cliché, if I am half the man my father is, my kids are going to be okay.

About the Author

Chuck Soltys is a 26-year law enforcement veteran. He is currently a federal agent and Tactical Emergency Medical Technician (EMT-B). He has been assigned to specialized enforcement groups as well as serving three tours of duty on a jungle operations team in South and Central America. Chuck currently serves as the

Primary Firearms & Tactics Instructor and is the coordinator of a Special Response Team. Chuck is an internationally recognized law enforcement trainer and author and has instructed extensively in the United States and abroad. Chuck is a 2010 Inductee into the Michigan State University School of Criminal Justice Wall of Fame.

Tougher than Woodpecker Lips

Ah-Hahs:

Take Aways:

Action Item:

Who are two people you consider to be mentors in your life?
Why? How have they influenced you?

I am Becoming That Man:
Let me tell you how he lived

By Jim Willis

> *"A chill runs along my frail frame. Through blurred vision and laboured breathing and pain there is a feeling...regret. As my heart slows there are flashes. Visions. Memories of choosing comfort, safety, security. False starts. Missed opportunities. Should have's. Sadness. With my last gasping breath I am left with one thought...I held back. I played it safe. I could have. I didn't. Regret. Blackness.*
>
> *I wake up. This is my greatest fear. My nightmare. That I will get to the end of my life and my last feeling will be regret. This is what drives me. This is what allows me to step to the edge and look into the unknown and close my eyes and jump."*

My nephew, Jesse Willis, penned those powerful and illuminating words in the winter of 2010, and as I read them they cut me to the core because these words so clearly described and defined the first fifty years of my life. It was a life that was great by any standard but it was a life that, to my regret, was played safely, that chose comfort over challenge, safety over risk, security over selflessness, convenience over sacrifice, and obscurity rather than courage. It was a life wherein many times I allowed my choices to be watered down or controlled or influenced by bullies; by people in power or authority; by fear of humiliation; by fear of failure; by my fear of people, thinking that if they knew the "real me" and all my flaws they would reject me.

For far too long I let the risk of disappointing people who were influential in my life define who I was and what I did. It took the death of four friends to help redefine and reshape my life. I then began the journey to truly live life to the fullest, the journey to becoming that man.

December 28, 2005 I received a phone call that would forever change my life. My good friend Derek, who worked with AIDS orphans in South Africa, had just died at age forty from a heart attack. Derek was the fourth friend in five years to die suddenly.

All four were great men and great friends. They were people I truly admired and respected. They challenged the status quo. They risked much. They loved much. They dreamed much.

When someone dies often the first question we ask is, "How did they die?" At the end of the movie *The Last Samurai*, the Emperor of Japan poses a question to Tom Cruise's character Captain Nathan Algren in regards to the samurai Katsumoto. The emperor simply states, "Tell me how he died." Capt. Algren responds with, what to me was a very powerful answer, "I will tell you how he lived." For too many of us it will not be until our eulogy is read that people will know how we lived.

As I looked back on the lives of these four friends who had died, I realized that how they lived was far more important than how they died. Their lives served as maps of how to live and what the journey can look like, and their deaths became marker stones for me as the road less traveled.

I decided that I wanted the impact they had on my life to carry on and be a living legacy of who they were. I wanted to be worthy of their influence on my life. As I thought about how I could begin to honor their legacies, I realized that all four had dreams of special things they wanted to do with their children but were cut short by their early deaths. So I started to dream about doing something big with each of my three children as part of carrying on their legacy. It had to be something that would be way outside of my comfort zone. Something that would be life impacting and life altering. Something that would stretch my faith to where I had to trust more than I thought I could. As Wallace and Gromit would say, I wanted to go on a Grand Adventure. I also wanted it to challenge my children's lives, their faith and their worldview.

So after much thought and discussion with my wife we came up with a plan. It should be noted, that year was going to be our 25th wedding anniversary and we had been planning something special to do as a couple. However, my beautiful wife said that planning the trips with our children was my gift to her. So I stepped to the edge, looked into the unknown, closed my eyes and jumped.

First, I took my then 11-year-old son to Romania and we lived at an orphanage. Talk about out of my comfort zone! We heard horror stories about children who had been abused and carelessly discarded and whose lives had now been transformed into stories of pure hope with a vision for the future because of the lives of people who risked and sacrificed much and loved these kids unconditionally. My son and I traveled to small, rural villages in Romania and we got to interact with families and children in the midst of poverty and lifestyles that probably haven't changed much over the past few hundred years. We brought donated funds and were able to provide 80 children from several villages with new running shoes. I will never forget the look of joy and excitement on those children's faces as they received their new shoes. It made me realize that our abundance in North America has numbed us to our own wealth as well to the needs of the world. I was so proud of my son, who even at that young age, was able to partner and share with me in that special journey.

In July of 2006 I took my then 18-year-old son and we traveled to Africa and climbed Kilimanjaro, the highest mountain in Africa. That was the hardest physical and emotional thing I have ever done, but what an amazing life event to share with my son. I will never forget standing on the summit of the Roof of Africa with my son. Absolutely glorious! We then traveled down to Mozambique to work with missionary friends for a week. It was a trip that was filled with trepidation; and at times great fear for me due to the language and cultural barriers, and more importantly the snakes, crocodiles and poisonous spiders. Someone once said, "Rather than trying to overcome your fear of snakes it is better to simply avoid them altogether." Well that wasn't a possibility where we were. Once again it was a life-changing event as we spent time amidst the poor, the widows and orphans, and the disenfranchised of the world. But again and again we saw people who were given hope for a new life because of the selfless sacrifice that our friends lived out every day. What an inspiration to be able to partake in that life if even for only a week.

Finally, my daughter was training that year to become a missionary pilot and she did all of her commercial pilot license training on float planes. So I went and flew with her for almost a month. What a blast and what a joy to share this time with my daughter and see her shine in her element as a pilot. She was amazing!

I believe that many of us probably think that our life story is not important enough to share with others. For me, these past five years have given me a new perspective on that idea. Those grand adventures laid a huge foundation for my life and as I have shared about my travels with my children, I quickly discovered that people were not only interested, but in turn they were challenged to reexamine their own lives. This time with my children definitely reshaped not only my life and faith but those of my children as well.

Over the past five years these adventures have given me a renewed courage to pursue my life with vigor, to share my faith boldly and to build relationships by taking risks. I am constantly reevaluating how I spend my time, money and resources and I am now willing to sacrifice and risk much.

I have been asked if I have any regrets in life, there was a time where my response was that I regret that I didn't live years ago like I am living now. But as I reflected on that statement, I have come to realize that I wasn't ready to live this way until now. It took all of my past experiences to form the foundation of what I am becoming. I have found that it is important to remember the things you went through because they serve to make you who you are today.

My brother, Brian Willis, always concludes his emails and correspondence with the following statement, "Take care and always remember Life's Most Powerful Question - What's Important Now?" As I ask myself that question many times a day, I sense that I am becoming that man that my friends' lives challenged me to become. I trust and hope that when the question is asked about me at my funeral, "How did he die?" my friends and family will instead be able to respond, "Let me tell you how he lived." Those I leave behind will be able to truly say it was a life that was worthy—that I was that man.

About the Author

James Willis is a Board Certified Ocularist and he has worked in the field of ocular prosthetics for 36 years. He has lectured to numerous medical and educational groups in both Canada and the United States. He has published several papers in both *The Journal of the American Society of Ocularists* and the *Journal of Ophthalmic Prosthetics* and has co-authored a chapter in the textbook *Advances in Ophthalmic Plastic and Reconstructive Surgery*. James is also a past senior editor of the *Journal of Ophthalmic Prosthetics*.

I AM BECOMING THAT MAN:
LET ME TELL YOU HOW HE LIVED

AH-HAHS:

TAKE AWAYS:

ACTION ITEM:

The Apple Doesn't Fall Far From the Tree

By Wally Adamchik

If I am that man, it did not happen by chance. As I approach my fiftieth year I know I am the sum of the impacts and efforts of many people. First among them are my parents. Coaches, teachers, bosses and others have all contributed, but they were only building on the foundation created by my parents. I realize in some ways I have lived up to what they all hoped for me, but deep inside I know there are some areas where I fall short. I am still growing. Yet, without these influences I would not be the person I am today. With these influences, I can be better tomorrow. That is an important message for all.

Mom and Dad

I remember my relationship with my Father as a very positive one. Interestingly, his father died when he was five so he had no male role model in his life. This meant that we didn't talk much about things. I am not sure he knew how to have those conversations since he never had anyone model it for him. So, when we did talk it mattered even more.

Things they taught me:

- If you have time to do it right the second time you had time to do it right the first time—yes this is a tired cliché but he believed it and used it. It established in me the need to practice hard and be prepared.

- Did you do your best?—Sports were big in our house and over the years I had my share of wins and losses. His universal comment, especially after a loss, was, "Did you do your best?" Of course, that extends beyond sports and it instilled in me the understanding and desire to leave it all on the field, to have no regrets.

- Nice day—this is about making a commitment and living up to it. This comment specifically related to my work as a caddy at a golf course during high school and college breaks. He would come into my room at sunup and simply say, "Nice day." What he really meant was, "Get up and go to work." Similarly, when I didn't feel like going to sports practice he told me I had to go. I didn't have to play but I needed to be there.

- Be aware —From where are the fire exits in the restaurant to what street I am walking down, he taught me to be aware. It was a cautionary lesson to help me stay away from trouble before it happens and how to get out of it if it does arise.

- You don't talk in front of your girlfriend like that, do you?—This has to do with respect. In my late teens, as I was becoming pretty salty with my language, I made a profane comment. Dad simply said, "Why do you talk like that? You are educated; you don't need to use those words. You don't talk in front of your girlfriend like that, do you? You never hear me talk like that in front of your mother." In fact, I only heard him curse twice in my life.

- Let your actions speak—My mother was a major force in the growth of women's sports in the 1970s. She was the first woman to referee in Madison Square Garden and she called the first Woman's National Championship game in basketball. This was the precursor to the current NCAA tournament. When she went to these early national tournaments, she would come home and tell us about the trip. This was a big deal. One of the things she always mentioned was the referees who talked too much in meetings, trying to make themselves look good. They never got selected for the final games. Mom did get selected and it was based on her on-court performance. This performance got her invited to the Olympics. My father was a fan of this too. He hated excessive celebrations on the field. He would simply say to let the scoreboard do the talking. Or to paraphrase Lou Holtz, when you get to the end zone, don't make it look like you have never been there.

My parents were good, gracious people who taught me the importance of hard work and doing my best—always. I guess that means their greatest gift to me was character. They were of the highest character and if I have the character they did, I will be fine.

Clearly, they did not do it alone. The concept of "it takes a village to raise a child" is true. Friends and family had a reinforcing impact on me. I say reinforcing because these people shared the same values with my parents. This underscores the importance of who you associate with. It is tough for you to be that man if you associate with people who are not able to be that man. Take the five friends test. Take a look around at who you would consider your five best friends. Although each one is unique, as a group they will share certain traits and characteristics. Their traits are your traits. If you don't like what you see, you may need to find some new friends. They are your village. My wife is number one on the list of five and in the things that truly matter we are in deep agreement. I learned this from my parents too.

The big question—am I that man?

Of course, as a father I now work to be that man. To be all the good things my children need. So, "upon further review" as the saying goes.

Me

This is a much tougher conversation as the story is still being written and I want it to be a good one. I have learned that my example is paramount. This is one of the foundational principles of leadership. In fact, I dedicated an entire chapter to setting the example in my first book on leadership, *NO YELLING: The Nine Secrets of Marine Corps Leadership You Must Know To Win In Business*. With that said, the first hurdle to being that man is to be everything listed above that my Father and Mother gave to me.

My gift to a son would be love, dirt, guns and a better example. Of course, what I really mean by that is to let him be a boy and to go do boy things. In fact, as I write this he is recovering from a broken arm, wrist, leg and ankle he got by skiing a tad too fast! My gift to my daughter would be love, dirt, guns and a better example. You have to know my daughter. She never took to Barbie dolls. In fact, we never owned one. What I am really saying is I must allow them to be themselves and not something I want them to be. I love my kids because they are unique, not because they fit a mold. Acceptance is a great gift. Another gift would be patience. It helps little when I get angry. In fact, it teaches anger. I have much work to do in this area. They frustrate me when they do not live up to their potential, but I also know this is part of youth and it gets right back to acceptance.

My advice to children is to be your own person. No one can tell you how to feel, and no one can know what you are feeling. No one should tell you what you need to do to be cool. You are already cool. Being you makes you cooler.

I have learned that being that man is not about being macho or using bravado. It is about being a partner and sharing the burden. I know many fathers who wouldn't dream of taking the kids for a weekend trip. They are missing out. We do it all the time.

As a man amongst men, I have learned that I am good enough. My experiences, learning, relationships and character combine to make me a man. Human, yes; flawed, yes; but just fine too. I have nothing to prove to anyone. Yet, I am a work in progress, which gives me energy and hope.

About the author

When you work with Wally Adamchik, you get the accrued knowledge of a lifetime dedicated to leadership and improvement. He is a regular presenter at construction industry events.

In his youth, Wally often worked with his father and brother in construction. Both master craftsmen, they insisted upon and produced top-quality work. He learned more about excellence from his mother, who was the first woman to referee a basketball game at Madison Square Garden. At the University of Notre Dame, Wally was the mascot where he led 65,000 people on every football Saturday.

As an Officer of Marines, Wally deployed throughout the world as a pilot of AH-1W Super Cobra attack helicopters. He was later recognized for superior performance and award-winning leadership at two national restaurant companies. At the same time he earned his Master of Business Administration from the University of North Carolina at Chapel Hill.

Today he is the President of FireStarter Speaking and Consulting, a national leadership consulting firm. He is a Certified Speaking Professional and a Certified Management Consultant. He continues to serve the Marines as a Non Resident Fellow with Marine Corps University. His book, *NO YELLING: The Nine Secrets of Marine Corps Leadership You Must Know To Win In Business* was selected as one of the best business books of 2007 by Entrepreneur magazine.

He no longer has any hobbies since he has two children under the age of ten.

The Apple Doesn't Fall Far From the Tree

Ah-Hahs:

Take Aways:

Action Item:

Pillars of Substance

By Chris Ghannam

After many years of deep self-reflection, I find myself forced into a continuous confrontation with a self-projected image of myself defined by an ideology. How does one adequately pay tribute to critical life experiences, past associations or personal and professional relationships? Have I repaid the many acts of kindness I have been so fortunate to receive? Why does it take a tragedy or the passing of a loved one, colleague or warrior to fully appreciate another's physical presence? How can a man's brief question ultimately re-align my personal and professional direction in life? I give credit to a series of conscious and subconscious comparisons I have created from interactions and relationships with those I consider: heart, courage, angel, mentor, life coach and hero.

Within every successful organization or family there is the heart, fueling the pulse behind motive, ambition and empathy. My mother is my heart, a living definition of selfless devotion. It is my mother's heart that enabled her to continue giving without breaking stride as she battled cancer. It is my mother's heart that gave her the strength to comfort her son through two wars. It is my mother's heart that showed me the place of origin for all righteous motives. It is my mother's heart that reaffirms what it means to have empathy for all those less fortunate, and it is that heart acting as a catalyst that drives my personal and professional ambitions in life.

One may assume I would attribute courage to a life lesson experienced over the course of two wars; however, my greatest lesson in courage came after my time in service. I learned that an experience can haunt a man for the rest of his life. The day I had to watch my brother Joe bury his son will never leave me. I will never forget the agonizing pain of watching my brother standing over a coffin shorter than arm's reach, symbolizing a life yet to be lived. I watched my broad-shouldered best friend and younger brother stand tall for his wife, son and family. He displayed a form of courage I couldn't compare to war, a courage that came without notice, without responsibility and without understanding. When warriors assume the duty of a first-line defender, they do so with the appreciation, responsibility and understanding for the inherited risks associated with the profession. They say a man's true character only shines in the presence of adversity. That day I learned that my brother Joe was the strongest man I have ever met.

I strongly believe that every man or woman has an angel; a special person in his or her life who has passed yet continues to look down upon them. That presence becomes readily apparent when a first-line defender faces a potentially dangerous or life-threatening situation. Many have experienced the chill running up their spines, and some associate that feeling with the notion of a sixth sense. For me, my chill was affirmation that my dear friend Benjamin Allen Johnson was looking over me. Ben was one of the first warriors to fall at the onset of Operation Enduring Freedom, during a search and seizure operation aboard an Iraqi vessel in the Persian Gulf on November 18, 2001. Ben sacrificed his life defending his country and remains a constant reminder of how fortunate we all are to be alive.

I have several amazing people that I consider personal mentors; however, none have affected me intellectually the way Mr. Jeffrey Norwitz has. Jeff is the quintessential world-class educator, a true warrior scholar. If I could emulate another educator, I would want to be Jeff Norwitz. His superior intellect summons the highest respect, and his passion is seen and felt through the delivery of his dynamic instruction. Beyond Jeff's unwavering and admirable integrity and devotion to duty is a rare human quality that I can't quite summarize in words. The level of respect he shows his wife, his thirst for knowledge, his quick-witted humor and his charismatic leadership are the personal traits I appreciate most. While the former will ensure Mr. Norwitz leaves a legacy never to be forgotten, it is the latter that demonstrates what it means to live a life of excellence.

Is it surprising the man I consider my personal life coach was the educator who requested a brief submission of my deepest thoughts? Brian Willis is known for asking, "What's important now?" After many years, Brian's question still resonates through every inch of my body. This question has the potential to not only alter perceptions, but also to re-align our very thought process for navigating this difficult road we call life. While "What's Important Now" may factually define life's most important question, the rationale behind choice represents its foundation. Through choice, an individual is given the latitude to assign a series of priorities to a given task, belief or action. Through choice, I am able to accept the errors of my ways. Through the tutelage of Brian Willis, I am able to choose to always ask myself the right question, "What's important now?" So how can one question ultimately re-align one's personal and professional direction in life? Simple really: have a world class life-coach ask the right question.

My late grandfather Sam "SARK" Ingesoulian is another hero, fitting for me to name SARK Securities in his honor. Frequently, a hero is denoted for how he or she paid the ultimate sacrifice. My grandfather is best remembered for how he lived his life, his many sacrifices and the standard he set for all who were fortunate to observe his actions. SARK was a World War II Army veteran, professional baseball player and boxer, feared by many, loved by most and appreciated by all who knew the man behind the stern face and cement-like hands. My grandfather's collectivist approach towards life ensured his family and colleagues were always given precedence. My grandfather eloquently demonstrated what it meant to be successful in business and life. He took on challenges most men would willingly shy away from. It is difficult for me to consider my grandfather a failure at anything. If he fell flat on his face, he would be up and running in the blink of an eye. When I was young, I often inquired about his success; he would say he was only halfway there. I did not fully understand my grandfather's wisdom until I was much older. He taught me that regardless of success, the final destination is of little importance without cherishing and respecting the relationships along the way.

In closing, I find myself stuck in a constant state of unreachable comparisons. I am both humbled and blessed to have so many influential factors help mold my future. Even though many of my personal aspirations may prove unobtainable, the beauty is that I have the choice to never surrender to the many challenges that lie ahead. For all who have and continue to support and believe in me, I am forever grateful.

About the Author

Chris Ghannam - Founder and CEO, SARK Securities Inc.

Chris Ghannam is denoted as one of the Defense Industry's most forward thinking trainers where his services have been contracted in a sole-source capacity by the U.S. Army, U.S. Air Force and U.S. Federal, State and Local law enforcement. Chris began his career in the United States Navy, quickly receiving top honors as the U.S. Naval Pacific Fleet Electronics Technician of the Year in 2002.

As the Global War on Terrorism commenced, Chris diverted all of his efforts towards the intelligence community, independently drafting 11 national level intelligence reports and assisting the Defense Intelligence Agency, CIA, FBI and National Geospatial Intelligence Agency in developing forty additional intelligence reports. He crowned his military career by identifying, detaining and exploiting one of the most senior Cuban Foreign Intelligence Service Agents ever held in U.S. custody.

Chris's research efforts have potentially produced the industry's first "patent pending" neuroergonomic weapon's technology with an official anticipated release date of 2012. Additionally, he was instrumental in the technical feasibility of a next generation surveillance technology that was awarded an SBIR contract, sponsored by the Office of Naval Research, funded by the Secretary of Defense.

The creator of "Project Achilles" an advanced neuro-kinetic development program designed to rapidly facilitate neuromuscular conditioning while mitigating cognitive overload in service members operating in hostile environments. A recognized world-class instructor, having lectured at some of the nation's most respected training venues. Chris has acquired expertise in the fields of security, counterterrorism, hand to hand combat, close quarters battle (CQB), HUMINT operations and urban warfare survival after having spent nearly six years abroad studying terrorist cells and advanced criminal networks.

Chris has been a project manager overseeing U.S. Government contracts for over five years, consistently receiving outstanding reviews on all assignments. He created the Southeast Regional Warrior Symposium, the Defense industry's largest closed-door training conference in the Southeastern United States and has acted in the capacity as lead consultant for a national level pre-meditated murder case involving a senior Special Forces service member—the military later reached a verdict of not guilty on all charges.

Chris Ghannam spends considerable time both orchestrating and fostering support for the warrior community to include the National Law Enforcement Officers Memorial Fund, SOF Care Coalition and Final Salute Inc. 501 (c) 3. Additionally, he writes for *PoliceOne* as an expert contributor in the areas of training transformation and homeland security.

Chris is currently pursuing his MBA at the University of South Florida with concentrations in Entrepreneurship, International Business and Management after having completed degrees with honors in Business Administration and Management, Applied Technology, Supervision and Management (Magna cum laude).

PILLARS OF SUBSTANCE

AH-HAHS:

TAKE AWAYS:

ACTION ITEM:

Not What the World Would Call a Hero

By Brian McKenna

My father was not what the world would call a hero. There are no streets or parks named after him, no lasting monuments to memorialize him, nor will his name ever appear in the history books. Still, in his own small corner of the world he did what he could to make the world a better place. He had no medals for conspicuous bravery, but I remember seeing a box full of combat ribbons when I was kid that belonged to him. They were ribbons he earned like so many others in the Greatest Generation had— by quietly doing his duty, not for glory but because his country needed him.

And like the others of his generation, he raised his children in the same unassuming manner. It wasn't his way to lecture or dictate; rather, he had a way of speaking and looking at you that made his meaning clear without any hint of disrespect or arrogance. No fanfare, just a quiet way of living that taught us right from wrong, respect for others, love of country, and the importance of family. As would be expected from a man like him, he possessed old-fashioned values long forgotten by many today like honesty, loyalty, hard work, commitment, and respect for the law.

All of these are important virtues for everyone to live by, but my father also taught us many things that apply more directly to law enforcement. Although he was a businessman, not a cop, he let it be known that his children were to respect the law and those who enforced it. There was no room in his world for disrespect, especially for someone who risked his life to keep others safe, and he would not tolerate it from any of his kids. It was this unwavering respect for police officers that first attracted me to the idea of going into law enforcement. My father also taught us an abiding respect for all people, not just those in authority. Again, he didn't lecture on the subject but just treated everyone that way. No one who knew Dad would doubt that even if he disagreed with them, he always respected them as individuals. I couldn't help but absorb much of that same attitude, and I'm convinced that it served me well throughout my law enforcement career.

Probably my father's greatest influence on my life and career was the attitude he conveyed about commitment and service to others. He used to say that "a man's word is his bond," meaning that when you give your word on something you will keep it no matter what. This applies to everyone who wears a badge because when we were sworn into office we promised to enforce the law, uphold the Constitution, and serve and protect our citizens. This is a tall order to fill, but thanks to my father I never lost sight of its importance or my solemn duty to fulfill it, whatever the cost.

Even more importantly, my father let it be known that there is no greater honor in life than to put yourself at risk in service to your fellow man. His Navy service in the South Pacific during World War II was his proudest moment, and he considered himself blessed for having had the chance to do his part. I think there's a lot to be said about that kind of attitude in police work. While the nature of the job makes it easy to develop a cynical view of the people we serve, we should never lose sight of the fact that the vast majority of our citizens are decent people. Most are law-abiding, except for an occasional traffic violation or other minor offense, and most just want to live in peace while providing the best they can for their families. They may not always like having us around, especially when our roof lights are flashing in their mirror, but when their world comes crashing down on their heads and there's nowhere else to turn, they call us. They count on us to keep them and all they hold dear safe, and when others look to us to keep their world from falling apart how can we say no? That's what Dad taught me and it's what police work is all about. It's about serving others regardless of the risk, about being part of something bigger than yourself and about somehow making a difference. It's also what makes police officers stand out above those they serve, even if those same people don't always appreciate it. Now as I look back over my 32-year law enforcement career, I can truly say that the thing I miss most about the job is the honor of being there for people who need me.

My father may not have been what many would call a hero, but he did his small part to make the world a better place. He willingly sacrificed his time and effort to provide for our family, and quietly passed on his time-honored values to us kids. Even more, like those of us who have had the privilege of standing in the Thin Blue Line, he made a difference by being part of something much bigger than himself.

Dad has been gone for about 25 years now, but I still think about him almost every day. It seems that every good quality I possess comes from him, not because he demanded it but because he showed me the way. I don't know if I am "that man," but I do know that I was a much better cop because he was such an influential part of my life. I'm a better husband, father and human being for having been his son.

About the Author

Brian McKenna is the owner of Winning Edge Training. He retired after 30 years with the Hazelwood (MO) Police Department. At the time of his retirement, he was assigned to the patrol division as a shift supervisor (lieutenant), and also served as an in-service trainer and lead firearms instructor. He is a state certified police instructor and former academy instructor, and holds a Master's Degree in human resource development. Brian writes extensively on officer safety topics, and authors *Law Officer Magazine's Officer Down* column, a regular feature that analyzes officer-involved shootings for key learning points.

Not What the World Would Call
a Hero

Ah-Hahs:

Take Aways:

Action Item:

"Situational Awareness" and the Creation of Character

By Mike Asken

> *I would rather people ask why no statue was erected in my honor, than why one was.*
>
> —Marcus Porcius Cato

The importance of mentors and models in shaping individuals and their life paths cannot be understated. In fact, such mentors are often immortalized in life and in fiction: trainer Mickey Goldmill developing a simplistic Rocky Balboa in Rocky; Glenn Holland crafting and shaping his students in *Mr. Holland's Opus*; or Coach Herman Boone barking and whispering life lessons to his athletes of raw potential in *Remember the Titans*.

Also important are the multitude of personal stories of appreciation and recognition from grateful individuals who have chiseled their character with the guidance of their mentors; many excellent examples are represented in this piece. I have often thought about such influences in my life. In my youth I called it reflection and now, later in life, realize it is reminiscence. But what has been disturbing to me is that I have never been able to identify a unique model of influence and impact for myself like so many others reverently describe. I often wondered if I have been unobservant and clueless or cheated in some way.

Certainly there are those that I admired. I stood in awe of Mickey Mantle and the Knights of the Roundtable (so much so that my oldest son was named after Sir Tristan). In the naïve haze of youth, such figures—real or mythical—were inspirational and without flaw. Youth is a good time for such adulation, a time before reality clarifies "the Mick" being awash in vices and the Knights rarely having washed. But the essence of nobility, achievement, excellence and other values were imprinted on my character.

Reflection and reminiscence has finally taught me that there need not be a single influence and that it is possible for a respected maturity to develop from contact with many individuals and engaging many experiences. My influences came from models who were real and also those that were fictitious. These influences occurred early and late and throughout life; occurred from individuals I knew personally and also those known only by reputation or work; occurred from those I could acknowledge and thank and from those who never knew of their impact on me. And in a curious way, while there were influences of which I was sharply aware, at other times I could only recognize their impact later or in different circumstances.

My father was a quiet man, my memories of who rarely consist of any direct instruction, coaching or teaching. Yet one of my strongest memories is of a eulogy at his funeral where he was described as a man of unfailing integrity. Those words created for me what gestalt psychologists call an "aha" moment, an instant of clarifying insight. Indeed, my father had always modeled and conveyed unfaltering integrity without ever speaking of it. He created for me a valued character goal in myself and a "holy grail" for which to seek in others.

A catalog of life values were illustrated and offered to me time and time again and in experience after experience. As I was not as fortunate as others to have a single north star pointing the way, I had to discern and decide personally on the values I would adopt to be the person I would become. I suspect that even with the most sage and sincere mentoring we all ultimately have to choose our path ourselves.

I once vehemently complained to and questioned my college advisor why I couldn't just take psychology courses and why I had to take what seemed to be many irrelevant studies like art history or anthropology. He responded that all knowledge is valuable and that one never knows when it might be critical. He further advised that if I were to indeed become a psychologist (apparently he had his doubts) I would spend the rest of my life studying and immersed in that topic. This, he said, was my best and maybe last chance to gain broad experience and sample things I may never have time to pursue again. He was right on both points.

Eric Greitens emphasized the value of diverse and seemingly incompatible experiences in his book *The Heart and the Fist*. Greitens is a very interesting individual who was a Rhodes and Truman Scholar and received a doctoral degree from Oxford University after graduating from Duke University. Involved in humanitarian work around the world for many years, he became a U.S. Navy SEAL and completed four deployments during the Global War on Terror. The salutary, if unexpected, merging of his seemingly opposite experiences and views is seen in his comments of being involved with both Nuns and SEALS.

> *"As warriors, as humanitarians they taught me that without courage, compassion falters and that without compassion, courage has no direction."*

I cannot recall every one of my transformational experiences, but several remain with me. When I was about eight years old, there was an exciting TV show that I would never miss called *Tales of Texas Rangers*. The show would open with the lead Ranger walking alone and determined down a dusty Texas street, only to have his fellow Rangers form a phalanx as they filled in behind him. I can still feel in my gut the sense of pride, loyalty, and nobility of protecting others that I imagined they felt.

I mentioned the subtle imprinting of integrity from my father; much less subtle were the lessons of compassion and service I learned from my mother. Later in life I learned much about human potential and possibilities from my children.

Many years were spent working on a hospital medical rehabilitation unit where I saw patient after patient, many quite elderly, all infirmed and inhibited by the ravages of a stroke, neurological disease or pulmonary decompensation work, strive and fight on a daily basis to move a few more inches or lift a few more ounces, just to get back to square one. What I learned there was about the resiliency and tenacity of the human spirit, as fervent and intense as in any Olympian display.

The many professionals I learned from, worked with or read from inspired motivation, the importance of excellence and how all satisfaction is ultimately amplified when these values exist in the context of helping others. When I became involved with law enforcement many years later, much of this was reinforced and augmented by the daily and sometimes exceptional and heroic demonstrations of commitment, dedication, selflessness, and courage by the Troopers and Officers.

I suppose the biggest lesson I learned from all this is that, while it is wonderful to have a lifelong Merlin or Dumbledore, it is not necessary. If we develop and maintain what in law enforcement and military we call situational awareness, we will find that every situation is developmental and edifying. But we have to have that situational awareness.

Micah Endsley, one of the leading experts in situational awareness, tells us that there are three points at which Situational Awareness is essential or can fail. The first is Perception: we fail to notice or perceive what is important. The second is Comprehension: we can fail to understand or recognize the importance of a situation. Finally, there is Projection: we can fail to make use of the information we have and we fail to project the knowledge onto ourselves and into our future. Hence, situational awareness is the key to character development if we are open and make use of it. It is instrumental in creating character that makes you into "that Man" rather than "that Guy" (a negative characterization often used by David Letterman to point out a striking or unusual individual of questionable merit).

There is a Pennsylvania Dutch saying that goes: "We get old too soon and smart too late." Don't let that happen to you. Stay aware and learn from everyone and every experience while making the best choices you can.

There is also a teaching, the source of which has now been lost to me, which counseled:

> *Anyone can learn from a wise man,*
> *but only a wise man can learn from everyone.*
> *Be that man or woman.*

References

Greitens (2011) Eric Greitens: *Leadership, purpose, inspiration.* www.ericgreitens.com/biography

Endsley, M, (2000). *Theoretical underpinnings of situation awareness: A critical review.*

In M. Endsley & D. Garland (Eds). *Situation Analysis and Measurement,* Mahwah, NJ: Lawrence Erlbaum Associates.

About the Author

Mike Asken is the Psychologist for the Pennsylvania State Police. He teaches at the State Police Academy. He is an instructor for the Pennsylvania State University's Commonwealth College.

Mike has presented training for the National Tactical Officers' Association, Memphis Police Department Command, the Texas Department of Public Safety, at the IACP, United States Postal Inspection Service, the FBI, Naval Special Warfare Group I SEAL Teams and the U.S. Army War College. He has published articles in *The Crisis Negotiator*, *The Tactical Edge*, The *Firearms Instructor*, PoliceOne.com, *Swat Digest*, *Law Officer*, *The Bulletin of the Pennsylvania Chiefs of Police Association* and the *FBI Law Enforcement Bulletin*.

He is the author of several books on the warrior mindset for police and military (www.mindsighting.com).

"Situational Awareness" and the Creation of Character

Ah-Hahs:

Take Aways:

Action Item:

Making the World a Better Place With the Gift of Time

By Kelly Hrudey

I'm not sure if we ever really know just why and when we are profoundly impacted by a single event that will guide us along the way for most our lives and maybe even determine who we are and how these events changed us.

My experiences growing up in Elmwood—a community in Edmonton, a very normal suburb on the west side of the city—had such an impact on my adult life because of the caring nature of the people living there and more importantly the volunteerism that was very prevalent. That's what really struck a chord with me.

I didn't start organized hockey until age twelve, and being on the brink of teenage years is what made me appreciate the actions of so many people in Elmwood.

For instance, I remember being blown away by the parents and volunteers that would scrape the ice for us before the games and practices (no Zambonis for our outdoor rinks in those days). Even more amazing were the volunteers that would stay and scrape and flood the ice for us late at night so that we would once again have a clean sheet of ice the next day.

It was no small task flooding the rinks either, since we had two regulation size hockey rinks plus a smaller rink for families to enjoy. Back then we would get huge snow storms, much larger and more frequent than today, and as kids we weren't strong enough to shovel the snow over the boards by ourselves; we needed the adults to help with the heavy lifting.

The other act of generosity that changed my life was the community board's policy to provide all the equipment free of charge for any kid who wanted to play goaltender in the league. The only thing they had to bring was their skates.

What a financial relief for so many parents! We all know the cost of equipment is high, even back then in the early seventies.

I don't remember every volunteer having a kid in the program; maybe they just knew the value the outdoor rinks in Elmwood had for the neighbourhood. The question I asked myself was, "Who does this type of stuff without a reward or compensation?"

Well, years later I learned the answer. We all can!

Ever since those amazing experiences with volunteerism, plus many others I've witnessed along my journey, I'm very proud to say I long ago joined the ranks of the many, many volunteers that make our villages, towns and cities a better place to live.

The beautiful thing about volunteering is that you can choose to help as much or as little as your schedule permits. The possibilities for volunteering are endless. You may enjoy being on a board or committee, adding your expertise in an area that the organization lacks. You may find that running the score clock at a rink fits your lifestyle better or selling raffle tickets or maybe even pouring coffee at a community event.

Recently I was on a flight to Toronto and while reading a newspaper I came across a special insert about a local Calgary Charity Golf Tournament from which they raised well over $300,000 in support of Prostate Cancer research. To raise this kind of money, there absolutely needs to be committees and volunteers.

The organizers recognized the value these people offered the tournament and the insert included a photo of the volunteers, 56 of them in total. Not pictured, but certainly not forgotten, were the 53 others who helped make the charity event a reality. That's right—109 people donated their time for something they believed in. What a rewarding experience for all of them.

This reminds me of a chance I had to visit Camp Horizon outside of Calgary, which is operated by Easter Seals Alberta. The camp provides a true camp experience for children and adolescents with cancer and/or other challenges. Camp Horizon also has a camp for young burn victims. As I chatted with some of the firemen from across Alberta that were volunteering, I was struck by their generosity. Not only do they donate their precious time, they do so while on their own vacation time. Incredible, isn't it? These amazing men and women spend their holidays cheering up youth that have been through traumatic and horrifying experiences, only to emerge more optimistic because of the help they are given from others.

These are people to look up to! I'm proud to say I've been the Honorary Chair for Easter Seals Alberta for the last few years.

A few years ago I was contacted by a couple of young entrepreneurs in Calgary about speaking to a group of their friends, all young successful businessmen, about how to get started with charity work. These young men knew of their early success in the business world but knew they had to do more to make Calgary a better place to live. They were stuck on how and where to start. I met with the group at the Calgary Petroleum Club along with the late Harley Hotchkiss. Mr. Hotchkiss was well known for his philanthropy, so his advice was very well received by the group. Harley and I spoke of ways to get started and shared some of our experiences. I was to discover later just how keen this group was to learn from a variety of different people; they've since included having T. Boone Pickens as one of their guests.

No task is too large or too small. Donating time is of the same importance as donating funds.

I look to a friend of mine that has the opportunity to do both. Entrepreneur and philanthropist, W. Brett Wilson, does a remarkable job of raising awareness and funds with all the resources he has to make Calgary a better place to live. Brett is also involved in many projects worldwide. Certainly Brett could simply write a few cheques and say he's done his part, but he personally likes to be involved with projects he's passionate about. He and many other charitable and compassionate people continue to inspire many regular citizens like you and me. It's important to never forget that no matter how busy and hectic your life may be, like Brett's, you can always find time to do something.

Luckily, I've been a part of so many different charity and community endeavours over the years that I can see and feel the impact they have had on me.

After retiring from the National Hockey League, one of my first experiences in Calgary was to visit the Tim Horton Children's Ranch in Kananaskis in 1999. This trip made me very aware that Canada has a serious problem of underfed, disadvantaged youth that are not leading the healthy lifestyle that they need. Now I volunteer for the Tim Horton Children's Foundation on a regular basis because they care so much about helping these kids and their families. They even have a youth leadership program that many of the campers take advantage of after their first experience with the camp. Many return for years, later becoming counsellors themselves, serving as mentors to the current group of campers.

For nine years, I hosted an event in Calgary called "Let's Talk Hockey" in support of the PREP Program (Pride. Respect. Empowerment. Program), a resource centre in Calgary that helps families that have children with Down Syndrome. I'm happy to say that because of everyone's generosity and hard work, we raised over one million dollars. Some of my guests that have donated their time, not accepting any money for their appearance, are Brian Burke, Bob Nicholson, Pat Laforge, Ken King, Bill Daly, Mike Milbury, P.J. Stock, Clint Malarchuk, Craig Conroy, Mike Cammelleri, Darryl Sutter and Brent Sutter.

I'm really proud of a new project that my wife and I find very fulfilling. It's one we call "PALS." This is not a large-scale project but one that is still very valuable. PALS stands for Philanthropy and Libation Society and I have to admit that I absolutely love this title. As a small group of six couples, we gather quarterly to discuss people in need and the best way to help them. Here's how our group makes its choice: Over a glass of wine or two, each couple tables a worthwhile situation involving a person or a family that they are passionate about and at the end of the evening we vote on the most pressing issue. We don't raise tens of thousands of dollars but I've learned that you don't have to do that to have an impact.

As the years have flown by and our children (Jessica, Megan and Kaitlin) are now all adults, it's so rewarding for Donna and I to see our children helping out in the community. Like us, they caught the bug and feel really good about their work in making our world a better place to live.

About the Author

Kelly Hrudey is a former NHL goalie and currently works as an analyst on CBC's *Hockey Night in Canada*. During his 15-year NHL career as a goalie with the New York Islanders (six years), Los Angeles Kings (seven years) and San Jose Sharks (two years), the former Medicine Hat Tiger compiled a record of 271-265-88, with a goals against average of 3.43 and 16 shutouts.

A popular and knowledgeable hockey commentator, Hrudey became a full-time hockey analyst with CBC'S *Hockey Night in Canada* during the 1998/99 NHL season after providing stellar commentary during the previous four playoff seasons with host Ron MacLean. In 2007, Hrudey was recognized for his work on the show with his first Gemini Award in the Best Studio Analyst category. He returns for his 13th season as an analyst with CBC'S *Hockey Night in Canada*, hosting *Coast to Coast* with Ron MacLean and Mike Milbury during the first intermission of Game Two of the Saturday night doubleheaders. The Gemini Award-winning analyst also joins MacLean and Scott Oake for the post-game show, *After Hours*.

In February 2006, Hrudey worked as an analyst for CBC's broadcast of TORINO 2006 – THE OLYMPIC GAMES, marking his second Olympic broadcast experience.

Fans can follow Kelly throughout the regular season and playoffs on Twitter at http://twitter.com/KellyHrudey

Hrudey resides in Calgary with his wife and three daughters.

MAKING THE WORLD A BETTER PLACE WITH THE GIFT OF TIME

AH-HAHS:

TAKE AWAYS:

ACTION ITEM:

The Banquet Speech

By John Dunn

When I was asked by Brian Willis to make a contribution to this book, I realized that the way I live my life and the way I perform my job have been influenced by too many people for me to single out one or two individuals who I could identify as my "primary mentors." In fact, when Brian told me about the book and the theme he was trying to address in the book—*am I that man?*—I immediately thought about a quote from the motivational speaker Stephen Covey: "begin with the end in mind." When we ask ourselves "Am I that man?" it is clear that we have a goal in mind of who or what we are striving to become. By asking this question, we force ourselves to reflect upon where we are as a person and where we want to go. The Cheshire cat in Lewis Carroll's classic novel, *Alice in Wonderland*, spoke with much wisdom when he said to Alice, lost in Wonderland: "If you don't know where you are going, then it really doesn't matter which road you take." *Going somewhere* is analogous to *becoming someone* in the context of asking ourselves "Am I that man?" The danger, of course, with living our lives in accordance with the Cheshire cat's philosophy is that we might become someone who we later realize is not the person we wanted to be! Had we begun with the end in mind or had we taken the time to ask ourselves, "Am I that man?" we would have had a much better chance of becoming the person we wanted to be!

For many years I have had the honor and privilege of working with elite athletes in the world of high-performance sports and also with the courageous personnel of various military and law enforcement communities. My primary role in these different performance environments has been to help individuals find a way to effectively function in highly stressful situations. Stated differently, I try to find ways to help performers find a mindset that allows them to (literally and figuratively) pull the trigger and hit the target at moments when hitting the target is the only option. There is no magic pill that allows individuals in these environments to "perform on demand." To the contrary, the factors that allow individuals and teams to excel under the most extreme pressure can almost always be traced back to how well they trained (physically, mentally, and emotionally) and to the types of actions they took on a daily basis that prepared them for these critical moments. More specifically, the "way we live" and the "way we prepare" have a profound impact upon our readiness to achieve the goal of action. As the old training philosophy so rightly states, "We must practice with a purpose."

One of the most powerful and effective mental-training exercises I have conducted with performers (including myself) for many years is called the "Banquet Speech." It is a simple self-reflection exercise that, when done properly, can create a roadmap for behavioral and attitudinal change, and can help performers answer the question, "Am I that man?" Here's how it works:

> Look ahead and imagine you are coming to the end of your career and you are being honored at a banquet. The only people who are present at the banquet are those individuals in your life who you most value: your family, your friends, your colleagues, your mentors. One of your most trusted friends is going stand up and talk about you at the banquet. That person will talk about all the great things you brought to the job, all the great characteristics and values that you demonstrated, and all the reasons why you became a role model for others. You would be willing to give almost anything to hear that speech; you might even be willing to give your life! Hearing the speech would be the proudest moment of your career!
>
> Now comes the interesting part. *You* get to write the speech that you would most like to hear at the banquet! You must put aside your ego and write the speech that would mean the most to you upon your retirement.

As a professional working with elite performers in multiple environments, I too have written this speech for myself. It has become my professional creed. It is the benchmark against which I evaluate my actions. I use it to hold myself accountable. I use it to guide and motivate my intentions. In essence, every day I look at my speech and I ask myself, "Am I that man?" I ask myself if I am living up to the behaviors and attitudes identified in my speech. I constantly have to ask myself if my speech describes the *real me* or the *me I want to be*?

As you will see below, I have included my banquet speech to give you an idea of what might go into your own speech. My speech describes the "person I want to be" as a practitioner who works with elite performers. My speech was not written in a day! It has evolved over the last 15 years as I have continued to work with elite performers in different environments. It is a fluid document and is constantly changing (although the basic principles seldom deviate). I know that I am running the risk of appearing to be arrogant and self-serving by using myself as my own role model in the context of this book; however, I must stress that almost all of the sayings, ideas, and principles listed in my speech come from experiences and lessons taught to me by the performers I have worked with or from the performance philosophies of successful people who have taken the time to write down the keys to success in their own achievement domains. As such, I have been inspired by the knowledge, resourcefulness, courage, integrity, and wisdom of others, and I have incorporated the lessons they have taught me into my own performance philosophy.

My Banquet Speech

> If something needed saying, John always said it, irrespective of how the individual (the player, the coach, or member of the support staff) receiving the feedback felt as a result of hearing John's words. Whatever words came out of John's mouth were always said with the intention of making the team better or making the individual do his/her job better. John always maintained that his job was not a popularity contest; he was willing to sacrifice friendships in order to

win championships. Having said this, John treasured the friendships that he did establish with the players and staff a lot more than the championship medals that now hang on his office wall.

John never let friendship stand in the way of doing what was necessary to help the team achieve its goals. John established some close friendships with many of the players and coaches on the teams he worked with, but "friendship" never interfered with his work. John treated every member of the team with the same degree of respect, and held every member of the team accountable for their behavior both within and beyond the competition environment. Irrespective of "player status" or "player seniority" (be it captain or rookie), John always said what needed saying, and always listened to whatever someone had to say.

His communication and leadership style can be captured with three simple values: he was direct, he was honest, and he was open. You always knew exactly where you stood with John, and when he was in situations that required him to confront athletes on disciplinary issues, he was careful to reprimand the behavior and not the person. He was successful in maintaining the respect and trust of the athletes, and he was successful in getting athletes to respond in a positive manner when holding them accountable because John lived by the most simple leadership principle: "People don't care how much you know until they know how much you care." He went out of his way to show that he cared about each individual he worked with.

His greatest communication asset was his ability to separate friendship from his professional role. He might scream at you one minute over a heated professional dispute then invite you out for beer and wings the next minute, as if nothing had happened, to chat with you about your family and work.

It might sound as though John enjoyed these confrontational moments with athletes or staff members. Far from it! He hated them! He actually dreaded them and often had to go well beyond his comfort zone to engage in them! However, he understood that in sport and in life, there are times and circumstances that require actions where "You don't have to like it, you just have to do it." Quoting Sir Winston Churchill, John lived by the mantra, "Sometimes it's not enough to do your best; sometimes you have to do what is required."

John never accepted mediocrity from himself nor from anyone else on the team. He recognized that perfection was not always attainable, but that the journey towards perfection demanded certain high standards that had to be met. He set his own personal standards high, and demanded a high level of commitment to high standards from everyone around him.

John constantly brought energy, intensity, and enthusiasm to the team. People fed off his never-ending pursuit of success. He was the poster child for the saying, "You can't kindle a fire in another person unless the flame burns bright within!"

John was effective because he built a foundation of trust with the players. Every single player on the team acknowledged that although John worked closely with the coaching staff, whatever was said in confidence to John never found its way back to the coaches. It was apparent that John's first loyalty was to the players. Having said this, he took pride in the fact that he never undermined or usurped the authority of the coaching staff.

John made mistakes, but when he made a mistake he was always willing to assume responsibility for his errors. More importantly, John learned from his mistakes and worked hard to ensure that the same mistake was never repeated. If the players were ever critical of John's performance or role on the team, he listened to what they had to say. Moreover, John never asked people to do things that he wasn't willing to do (or hadn't done) himself. If he ever asked players to stand up in front of their teammates and answer critical questions about their performances and behaviors, John would also stand up and give the players an opportunity to provide feedback regarding his performance.

John always believed in dealing with problems head on. He never attempted to "brush things under the carpet" or "turn a blind eye" in hopes that problems would eventually sort themselves out. To quote the bad guy in Steven Segal's movie, *Dark Territory,* John firmly believed that "Assumption was the mother of all screw ups."

John's door was always open to the athletes when they needed to talk to him, whether the issue related to their sport, personal circumstances, or work. He'd do whatever it took to help an athlete stopping only when he felt that he would do something that would compromise his professional credibility or his own personal values.

John never believed that he or the athletes he worked with were there just "to make up the numbers." He believed that every team and every athlete had the potential to be successful. From John's perspective, participation in a competition meant that you were there to win, no matter how much the odds were stacked against you. Having said this, John never advocated a "win at all costs" attitude. Success and victory were to be earned with hard work, sacrifice, dedication, discipline and thoughtful planning. John always said, if you showed up for a competition, you were there to compete and to give everything you could. But John never judged people based upon the outcome of the competition. He judged people on the basis of their actions, their attitude, their commitment, their effort, and their support for their teammates.

John's commitment to the teams he worked with is best captured by his personal life philosophies, "There are no 'What If's'" and his 7 P's: "Prior Planning and Preparation

Prevents Piss Poor Performance." As a result, John rarely failed to perform! How many times did we hear him quote Lt. Col. Dave Grossman, "You don't rise to the occasion; you sink to the level of your training." For John it was always about preparation. When the team won, there was no one happier than John. When the team lost, there was no one unhappier than John. You always knew that John was fully invested from an emotional perspective in the team.

As John Wooden once said, "Sport does not build character; sport reveals character." John's character was evident in everything that he did and said as a supporting member of the team. He earned every word of this speech through his actions. Stealing from the words of Eleanor Roosevelt, "We can only hope that when John dies, he dies in his sleep, because if death comes for him during his waking hours, there is sure to be one hell of a fight."

DEEDS, NOT WORDS!

Having read my banquet speech, I hope you have been able to get a sense of how I use it to evaluate and to inspire my performance, and how I use it to provide a road map that steers me along the path I have chosen to walk. I wish I could say every day I read my speech that "I Am That Man," but that is simply not the case! There are times when I fall short of the man I aim to be. However, through honest (and at times painful) self-reflection and self-evaluation, I use my speech to direct my efforts towards improving my shortcomings and to build a reputation I (and others) will be proud of!

In preparing this manuscript, I gave a preliminary draft to my friend and fellow-contributor, Master Warrant Officer Willy MacDonald. I asked Willy for his honest feedback about the things I'd written and instead of giving me suggestions he simply asked, "Are you that man in the speech who is so highly regarded professionally and admired personally? Are you that man in the speech whose loyalty to subordinates was balanced by professional requirements? Are you that man in the speech who has been forged by your interactions with the *elite, the professional*, and *the morally strong* men and women with whom you work?" I am proud to say that my answer to Willy's questions was a resounding, "Yes (most of the time)!"

I encourage you to consider writing your own banquet speech and to challenge yourself to "become that man." It may be one of the best investments of your time that you ever make! You'll never know unless you try! There is, however, one important caveat to consider as you create your own banquet speech, "It's better to be a first rate version of yourself than a second rate version of someone else!" It takes courage to commit in writing (through your banquet speech) to define the person you want to be because in writing your speech you are accepting that every time you consider your speech you must answer the question, "Am I Really That Man?"

About the Author

Dr. John Dunn is a Full Professor in the Faculty of Physical Education and Recreation at the University of Alberta. He specializes in the area of sport psychology. John has published many papers in the world's leading sport psychology journals and frequently speaks at research conferences around the world. In addition to his research expertise, John is recognized for his contributions in the field of performance psychology where he has worked as a consultant and as a member of integrated support teams for a variety of athletes/organizations in Canadian Olympic and professional sport. He has worked with athletes and teams that have achieved victory at the provincial, national, and international levels of competition (including two world champions) and has spoken on a number of occasions to leading figures in the Canadian sport system at the invitation of the Canadian Olympic Committee and "Own The Podium." He is most proud of the performance enhancement work he has conducted with various groups within the Canadian Armed Forces and Canadian Law Enforcement communities.

THE BANQUET SPEECH

AH-HAHS:

TAKE AWAYS:

ACTION ITEM:

Identify one person in your life who you will make a commitment to mentor. List at least two things you will do to become a *trusted counselor or teacher* to that person.

She Sees my Dad in Me

By Floyd Colón

How often have you heard someone say, "When you get older, you won't have much of a future, but you will have many wonderful memories"? Or how about, "The apple doesn't fall far from the tree"?

In my case, those statements are surprisingly accurate! At the age of 72, I find myself reminiscing and remembering my past more and more. I was born and raised in Puerto Rico, and my family migrated to the United States when I was five-and-a-half-years old. What wonderful memories I have of a converted military troop ship bringing my family to "the promised land." My Dad wanted to provide the best for his family, and although he loved his homeland, he believed the United States was the best place for his family to prosper. We settled in Lincoln, Nebraska in 1947 and my life, as I know it, really began at that time.

One of my first memories of my Dad occurred when I was seven years old. We were in our home listening to the radio (television was non-existent at that point) and I said to my father, "Dad, do you want to play catch [baseball]?" My Dad loved baseball. He was recognized as one of the finest baseball players to ever play in the Puerto Rican winter league. The Brooklyn Dodgers offered him a contract when he completed high school, but he chose to further his education because he always believed that his future would be built on his education. How right he was! The first time I asked Dad to play catch with me, my baseball and life's education began. No matter how tired my Dad was when he came home from work, he would always respond to my request to "play catch." From my father came my love for baseball. I loved it so much that I named my two sons, Mickey and Charlie, after Mickey Charles Mantle. My sons played college baseball and semiprofessional baseball, and I can honestly say they inherited their talent from my father.

When we arrived in Lincoln, Nebraska, Dad could speak both Spanish and English fluently. He taught himself English as a youth in Puerto Rico. He began his drive for additional education when he registered to study for a master's degree at the University of Nebraska. I still remember Dad when he would attend classes at the University of Nebraska, and as soon as he finished his final class for the day, he immediately went to his part-time job as a "soda jerk." Yes, he worked behind the counter of a drug-store selling food and drink items to the customers. Dad always felt that any honest job was an honorable job, and Dad would accept any honorable occupation that would support his family and put bread on the table. Dad successfully completed his master's degree program and immediately began planning his doctoral degree. I would be remiss if I did not mention my mother at this point. Mom supported my Dad in his quest for higher education, working eight hours a day, five and often six days a week. Dad would be the first to admit that he could not have accomplished all that he did in his life without the support of his wife, my mother, Mimi. They were married 62 wonderful years and loved each other always.

After receiving his Master's Degree, Dad applied and was accepted for the position of Spanish Professor at Nebraska Wesleyan University. Dad received his Doctoral Degree while holding the position of Dean of Admissions at Nebraska Wesleyan. When he began his tenure as Dean of Admissions in 1954, Nebraska Wesleyan's enrollment was approximately 850 students. When Dad resigned from Nebraska Wesleyan in 1972, Nebraska Wesleyan's enrollment was just over 1500 students. I still meet people who say to me, "Your Dad recruited me to come to Wesleyan" or "Your dad was the reason I attended Nebraska Wesleyan." My father was a real people-person and touched so many lives. He cherished his friendships and I believe he passed that legacy on to me. After his retirement, Dad and I spent much time together discussing his memories. He advised me and he counseled me about everything including fatherhood, how to interact with people and that family is the most important thing in one's life.

Dad's family always came first. As an adolescent, I remember the sacrifices he made for us; when I thought I needed the most up-to-date fashions in high school he would spend the money. Dad always provided for his wife and his two sons first. He supported me through all of my athletic endeavors in high school and college without hesitation. He tutored and counseled me when I was attempting to make a decision about a career. And, as usual, he was always right in his assessments. When I graduated from college, I began a career with the Nebraska Department of Labor and it lasted 42 years.

Dad loved music, and he loved and lived his religion. Dad organized his own "dance band" while living in Puerto Rico. When he moved to Lincoln, he played in several "dance bands" in Nebraska. Dad was so musically talented that he could play many instruments by ear (that is, to play without reading the music). Once again my dad influenced me. I played in my high school band and helped form a rock and roll band while I was in college at Nebraska Wesleyan.

Dad always encouraged us to attend church regularly, and I have passed that encouragement on to my sons and their families. Religion plays an important role in the Colón household.

Then I married my wife, Fran, and we began our family. Our two sons called my dad "Papo," and along with my brother's three sons, became the loves of his life. Dad felt he could just never do enough for his family, let alone his grandchildren. "Love" was the key word in dad's relationship with his family. "Love" is the legacy that he left me with which to build my family. However, I must admit the fact that "love" was tempered with discipline. Dad always believed that relationships were founded and built on love and discipline. How right he was. My father passed away in 1996 and I lost my best friend. But Dad left me with the one thing I will always treasure… my memories of him.

I played, coached, and umpired softball for 38 years. I umpired high school baseball, legion baseball, and semiprofessional baseball for fifteen years. I coached semiprofessional baseball for sixteen years. I was inducted into the Nebraska Softball Hall of Fame in 1994, I was inducted into the Nebraska Baseball Hall of Fame in 1994, and I was inducted into my high school Athletic Hall of Fame in 1999. I was and I still am truly humbled by these awards, and I am unsure that I really deserved them. However, I am very proud of the recognition.

So now I have my wife, Fran, two sons, four grandchildren who call *me* "Papo," and they have all become the loves of my life. As you can see, I love baseball at all levels—small fry, high school, college, and professional. I hold dearly the memories when my sons used to ask me, "Dad, do you want to play catch?" It is true that what goes around comes around. Oh, the memories!

My wife tells me now that I even walk like my Dad used to walk. What a wonderful compliment! Dad was my hero and to be compared to him in any way is something I will always cherish.

My wife, Fran, often tells me that she sees my dad in me. I like to believe that I fell right at the trunk of the tree and never strayed any farther than that.

About the Author

Floyd Colón was born in Ponce, Puerto Rico, and has resided in Lincoln, Nebraska, since 1947. He earned a Bachelor of Arts degree in Psychology and Sociology from Nebraska Wesleyan University. Floyd worked for 42 years for the Nebraska Department of Labor in Lincoln retiring in 2004 as a research analyst supervisor. During his career he was an author and instructor in *"Supervision: An Extension of Management"* and participated in fifteen multi-regional seminars. Floyd was a quarterly presenter of his highly acclaimed presentation *"Thermostats and Thermometers"* in the Career Education classes in the Lincoln Public Schools, as well as at the University of Nebraska, several businesses, and several state agencies.

Floyd and his wife, Frances, who is a retired high school teacher, have two sons, Charlie and Mickey, who are both with The Gallup Organization. They also have two daughters-in-law, Dawn and Kelli, and four grandchildren, McKynzie, Cooper, Jalyn, and Kyndal.

Floyd is active in the Fellowship of Christian Athletes, his church and sports. He has coached semipro baseball, slow pitch softball, and assisted with his grandchildren's teams. He is an avid New

York Yankees fan and is a co-founder of the Nebraska Yankees baseball fan club, as well as a collector of Yankees memorabilia. He was inducted into the Nebraska Softball Hall of Fame in 1994, the Nebraska Baseball Hall of Fame in 1994, and the Lincoln Northeast High School Sports Hall of Fame in 1999.

She Sees my Dad in Me

Ah-Hahs:

Take Aways:

Action Item:

A Reflection on My Mentors

By Ian McRobbie

In everyone's life there appear people who shape, through intent or simply by their actions, our lives and who show us how to be the best that we can be. Whether we have internalized their example, and to what degree, determines the extent of that individual's influence in our lives. Of course, we each have many, many influences: our parents, siblings, spouses, teachers, coaches, bosses, coworkers and friends. We draw strands of the qualities we respect and wish to emulate from each of these, eventually weaving them, if we are focused and fortunate, into the person we wish to become.

I would cite my parents as my greatest inspiration and influence.

A nurse by training, then a homemaker by choice, my mother poured herself fully into the lives of her children. Driving, sewing, crafting and filling out reams of paperwork as swim team manager, she put the activities and interests of her children ahead of everything, including sleep! She has always possessed a remarkable capacity for remembering detail; whether it is a birth date or someone's likes and dislikes, she can produce these facts many years later. She puts this gift to use in many ways, most often by recalling with pride one of her family or friend's good qualities. She is always positive when speaking of others and finds a laudable quality, no matter how difficult that might be. She attends to the details of any task she takes on, and will never quit until something is the best that she can make it. Even now, past her mid-eighties, she brings this commitment to her volunteer pursuits, putting in countless hours of charity work at a stage when others might be content to hang up their smock. She has always possessed such a strong sense of loyalty to family, to work, to any commitment she has made, that to display even a portion of this would put one in rare company. The value she places on family and the efforts she makes to keep us all connected, regardless of the distance, are perhaps her greatest legacy. Our family is strong because of the ties she helps us maintain. Her love and pride are obvious, and knowing that she speaks of all of us with that same fierce pride is a key to how we have had the confidence to live such successful lives. By success, I mean not material possessions, though none of us lack for those; but happy, content lives, blessed by loving, caring relationships. Her calm, sage wisdom is a rock to which we are all anchored. She has seen and experienced much in her life, and while she will never force her guidance upon you, she has a wealth of wisdom to draw from if you ask for it or recognize it woven between the lines of conversation.

My father, too, is a huge influence in my life. I am pleased to see in myself so many aspects of his personality. For starters, the place which physical activity holds in my life is drawn from watching the positive effects it has had for him. I know the calming, stress-relieving effect daily exercise has always had for him, and seek this out in my own day-to-day life. Like my mother, he is a detail-oriented person in matters of work or crafts. He will often comment that his projects are over-engineered, but they never fail due to a lack of planning. In fact, they rarely fail at all. I think his creative solutions to challenging problems are an element of his character that I most enjoy discovering within myself. Regarding the details of everyday life, however, he tends to go with the flow, leaving minor things like times and places to my mother. He is a tireless and selfless volunteer, finding himself perennially in that 10% of people doing 90% of the work, yet continuing to step up because "somebody has to." Another of his qualities that I admire is his unquenchable quest for knowledge and personal growth. Into his eighties, a time when one could feel content to let their drive wane, he still reads calculus texts and a wide range of how-to work materials that keep his analytical mind from losing its edge. His woodworking pursuits are another example of how he continually tries new challenges to keep his interest fresh and his skill set growing. That same curiosity extends to his reading on religion and spirituality. A life-long churchgoer, he spent some time in his middle age assessing and weighing the attributes and appeal of many of the mainstream denominations. While the journey eventually led back to the same church, the quest certainly had value for him in verifying the correctness of his choice. His quest showed me that it is not only acceptable but actually very valuable to question our path and examine alternatives. I strive to emulate his laid-back, go-with-the-flow lifestyle. He is happy, upbeat and relaxed, easily finding the humor in any situation and using it to keep tensions low.

To be raised in this home seems now to be my life's greatest gift. Between the two of them, my parents provided us with an environment where accomplishments were celebrated, but not demanded, where we were free to pursue almost any path, knowing we would be loved and accepted regardless of the outcome. They instilled in each of us the confidence to try new experiences. They also kept the home full of laughter, love and positive energy, a lofty goal for any parent.

Another major influence in my life is my brother-in-law/boss/ coworker/friend, Jim. As well as teaching me the technical skills required to work in my profession, he has modeled the virtues of caring, compassion and patience in his dealings with people. In both his work and private lives, he will put a planned schedule aside if he senses that someone needs a sympathetic ear or caring shoulder to share their burden. I can cite countless times when a short appointment has stretched into a long session of someone unburdening their pain and struggles. His caring for these people provides them with a much-needed outlet for their issues, even though it can leave him burdened with their pain. Another of his attributes is the fierce pride he feels in the accomplishments of his children, family and friends. He is always quick to make people aware of the strengths, attributes and accomplishments of those within his circle of family and friends. He is a man of great faith and great humor, with a giving spirit and a strong moral compass. I am blessed to have had the benefit of his influence and friendship in my life.

Like many of us, I haven't really spent much time reflecting upon or assessing my success at living up to the ideals of my mentors. I've been busy caught up in the day-to-day whirlwind of work and family. Were it not for the opportunity presented by writing this article, I may never have stopped to reflect on these things. If our mentors are successful and we strive, even unconsciously, to emulate their excellent examples, we will be kind, loving, productive people who love both our families and our work.

This process has shown me certain commonalities in the people I admire: empathy, volunteerism, compassion and commitment. Oft-used terms maybe, but obviously attributes I value greatly. The mission for the next chapter of my life will be to become more deliberate about finding and sharpening these qualities in myself.

About the Author

Ian McRobbie is an ocularist (maker of custom artificial eyes) by profession. He attained a certificate in Biological Sciences technology from the Northern Alberta Institute of Technology, and then worked at the University of Alberta for seven years as a technician in a Multiple Sclerosis research laboratory. In 1988 he began his training as an ocularist, becoming Board Certified in 1993. He has served as associate editor of the *Journal of Ophthalmic Prosthetics*. He lives in Edmonton with his wife and their two children and enjoys running marathons and competing in triathlons.

A Reflection on My Mentors

Ah-Hahs:

Take Aways:

Action Item:

Identify at least one person you will reach out to and thank for their positive influence in your life.

The Most Important People You Can Honor are Your Parents

By Aaron Davis

> *We never know the love of the parent until we become parents ourselves.*
>
> —Henry Ward Beecher

Be Grateful for Your Myles and Martha

The words on this page could never express the love, appreciation, and respect that I have for my parents. Myles and Martha Davis taught me that I could do whatever I set my mind to, provided that I kept my faith in God. Even as a young boy running around our dirt-covered yard (with six kids, grass was a foreign object), my parents instilled in me the value of integrity, hard work, and a tenacious attitude!

The lessons that I learned at our dinner table have formed the bedrock of who and what I am today. I am definitely not perfect (my wife Brooke will tell you that), but I try daily to be all God would have me be. I learned the value of traveling the road less traveled from my father, Myles Davis, long before I read the famous poem, "*Road Less Traveled,*" by Robert Frost.

Growing up, athletics was a huge part of my life. I grew up playing basketball at the Malone Community Center and the Salvation Army Community Center in their Small Fry basketball program. Across the street was Pentzer Park where I played football and softball almost daily in the summer.

As I look back on those "good ole days" I remember each kid having huge dreams of one day playing in the NBA or the NFL or running on the field in front of 76,000 fans at the nearby University of Nebraska Cornhuskers Memorial Stadium. In fact, on home game days all of us neighborhood kids would be playing football, and during our games we would hear the roars of the crowd only a few miles away cheering on our beloved Cornhusker football team. It was those cheers and dreams that my parents encouraged me to pursue with passion and fervor!

My father was the quintessential man who took the road less traveled. In 1963, he moved his family to a predominantly white Lincoln, Nebraska, in search of a safer environment to escape the unforgiving and mean streets of Pittsburgh, Pennsylvania. It was from my dad that I learned the value of hard work and to never depend on any program or system to determine how far I could go in life.

My dad is a man of few words who always wears a smile that could shatter any obstacle that stands in his path.

I learned grit and determination from a lady that stands barely five foot two inches tall (but we all know that dynamite comes in small packages). My mom would never allow me to hang my head after a poor performance on the field or in the classroom. She would encourage us to learn from it but wouldn't ever allow our heads to drop in defeat no matter what the score or grade was. She instilled in me that each of us has the final say on the score if we only keep pressing ahead.

My parents are the reason that I am who I am today, and I thank God daily that I was given the chance to grow up in a home where both of my parents were active in my life. Any mistakes I've made, I could never attribute to them. Any success I've enjoyed, it was my parents who planted the seeds of possibility.

As I've gotten older it scares me to think about where my life would be today without my parents' love, direction and discipline. I can recall numerous times (I definitely tested my parents' patience more than a few times) where the hammer of discipline was exercised on me!

My parents were old-school and at the time I didn't understand it; however, I'm eternally grateful for it. For instance, growing up in my house you addressed adults by Mr., Miss or Mrs. It was never by their first names. To my parents it was and still is "Yes Sir" and "No Sir," "Yes Ma'am" and "No Ma'am." To this day I would never call any of my former teachers or coaches by their first name. My parents taught me something that I think is terribly missing in today's youth culture towards adults: RESPECT!

I encourage you to thank "your" Myles or Martha who helped shape and mold you. Maybe it was a teacher who saw something within you that you struggled to even see yourself; perhaps a coach that took you under their wing so that one day you would develop your own wings. No matter who it was, thank them and do it often.

Any success you enjoy today or have enjoyed or will enjoy in the future wasn't just by your own efforts alone; rather it was the collective influences of others who—like Myles and Martha—nourished, praised and encouraged me to be all that I was born to be!

About the Author

Aaron Davis speaks about performing like a champion from personal experience. He has shared with over a million people in the US and abroad about having the "Attitude of A Champion." As a member of the 1994 National Championship Nebraska Football team and working with numerous corporations and organizations, he understands firsthand what it takes to perform like a champion and experience incredible results both personally and professionally!

Aaron is not just a speaker "telling" other companies and individuals how to succeed. He's in the trenches everyday as the President of his own Consulting Firm ADP, Inc. and the partner in two other successful companies: www.greenbein.com, a media production company that specializes in adding digital interaction to existing marketing efforts that increases engagement, acquisition and revenue for their clients; and www.boxwire.com, a virtual suggestion box used by some of today's top companies to receive feedback from both customers and employees.

He's authored three books and has received numerous awards. He's married to his wife Brooke and they have two sons, Aden and Keenon, and a daughter named Niya.

The Most Important People You Can Honor are Your Parents

Ah-Hahs:

Take Aways:

Action Item:

Accomplishment:
How Much Is Enough?

By William MacDonald

To honour those that have been most influential in my life, I must begin with a story that changed the way I thought about the people around me.

It was 8:00 A.M. and I was told not to leave my office until further notice. Having been in trouble a number of times in the past, I wracked my brain trying to figure out what juicy little episode was coming back to haunt me yet again. It was August 13, 2009.

I decided it couldn't be something bad based on the demeanour of my boss and a few other colleagues. When I was finally called out of my office by my Battalion Adjutant I was asked, "Do you know what this is about?" I replied, "No, Sir!" and was taken up to the command cell offices. The Commanding Officer's EA was asked to transfer the call and I was told to go into the CO's office to take a phone call. Needless to say, I was somewhat confused. I answered the phone and was greeted by Lieutenant General Andrew Leslie, the Chief of the Land Staff (The Army Commander for Canada).

I knew Lt.-Gen Leslie from the Army Ball six months ago where I attended as the personal guest of Chief Warrant Officer Wayne Ford, the Army Sergeant Major. I was selected as CWO Ford's personal guest due to the fact that I had recently been awarded the Star of Military Valour, the second highest decoration for valour in the face of the enemy that the Canadian Forces can award, next to the Victoria Cross. The award was for a battle that occurred in Afghanistan on August 3, 2006, in which a small 14-man force of soldiers, including myself, were surrounded and cut-off by an estimated 175 enemy at an objective called "The white school." We lost four outstanding comrades that day (Sgt. Vaughan Ingram, Cpl. Chris Reid, Cpl. Bryce Keller and Pte. Kevin Dallaire) and another seven were injured. When asked about what I had done to deserve this decoration my answer was usually, "I survived."

During our telephone conversation, Lt.-Gen Leslie said to me, "Warrant MacDonald, I have good news. You've been selected as the 2009 Vimy Award recipient." I was speechless. Since I wasn't entirely certain what the Vimy Award was, I did not understand what it meant to be the recipient. He pushed on, "There are a few people here who would like to speak to you, can you hold the line?" Since it was Lt.-Gen Leslie calling, I figured it was a prestigious award and I waited patiently on the line. I then spoke to the Chief Justice of the Supreme Court of Canada, The Right Honourable Beverly McLachlan, followed by several other people who represented the Conference of Defence Associations Institute and then again Lt.-Gen Leslie before the call was ended.

I immediately researched the Vimy Award and was shocked to find that not only was I the only Non-Commissioned Officer ever to be selected, but the only serving member under the rank of Brigadier General. The other recipients included intellectuals and politicians; I was just a kid from Saskatchewan who was a mere Warrant Officer in the Canadian Infantry. The Conference of Defence Associations Institute presents the Vimy Award annually to a single Canadian who "has made a significant and outstanding contribution to the defense and security of our nation and the preservation of our democratic values." It was a good year for me.

I never really feel comfortable with being branded as a "hero" and I was even more uncomfortable with what I thought the Vimy Award would bring my way. It was then that I began to reflect on my life and my achievements, as well as call a few of my former and current colleagues for advice.

I thought of people like Adam Corbett and Johnny Devine, two of my most cherished friends, trusted confidantes, mentors and former supervisors. It's hard to swallow that you are the one guy who is picked from thousands to represent the institution, yet when you enter a room with those two you become the "little brother." Feeling overwhelmed by their knowledge and confidence, and in awe of the fact that these two had the biggest impact on my development as a soldier, naturally leaves a feeling of guilt in its wake. "Why not them?" I asked myself over and over. Certainly Adam and Johnny aren't the only two I could mention, but they are undoubtedly the most significant. How do you represent yourself without mentioning those who shaped whom you have become?

I also cannot forget my mother, Ma, who taught me perhaps the most important lessons of all. Be yourself, be unique and take the best of others in order to be a better you. Ma never did speak those words to me, but she lived them and her example and silent lessons were never lost on me. I cannot mention her without mentioning her partner, Wendy. Wendy is indeed a gentle soul who is loyal to a fault, reflective and will provide the advice you need without you having to ask. My mother left my father when I was less than a year old. We went to live with Grandma Doris, a strict disciplinarian, tireless lesson-giver and very, very loving in her own way. I once asked her why she was so hard on me when it came to chores and other tasks she would give me to complete. Her answer was simple, "If I demand perfection from you, you will achieve excellence." So it came to be that I was raised surrounded by women (I lived with Ma, Wendy, Grandma, my sister and a female dog named Emma). Perhaps that's what attracted me to a predominantly male line of work and why I have such smooth skin! It's probably also why I have absorbed the lessons they taught me tirelessly through their actions, silently shaping me in my most formative years.

The day that I was to receive the Vimy Award in November 2009 at a Gala reception held at the Canadian War Museum in Ottawa, I was called to a meeting with the Chief of Defence Staff for the Canadian Armed Forces, General Walt Natynczyk. He asked to see me to make sure that I was confident in being the recipient and to make sure that my nerves were in the right place. I have to say that although it was not the first time I had met him, he struck me, again, as a very impressive person. He is very charismatic, a great leader and a person who inspires others to be just as humble and confident as he is. The one thing I remember most is when I told him that there were folks in the organization who had said to me, "You know you need to change. With this award comes responsibility and you need to live up to that." General Natynczyk said to me, "Warrant MacDonald, don't listen to those people. You need to *not* change. What brought you to this award is who you are and the way in which you represent our Forces. This award is proof that you have already lived up to expectations." I took that to heart and delivered my acceptance speech that evening with confidence that I would know how to proceed after the award.

I have been given some great opportunities in my life and my career. Along the way, I have learned from the very best and been fortunate enough to have a wonderful family and some exceedingly great friends and mentors. Folks like Corporal Jamie Sinclair, the toughest little devil ever to wear a uniform (certainly the most proficient Corporal I know and a great teacher) and Major Jon Hamilton, an exceptionally competent and passionate combat leader, whom I followed through our Afghan mission and numerous engagements with the enemy.

At the end of the day, I sum up my accomplishments like this: "I would gladly give up the recognition and the memories, if it meant I could have Vaughan, Bryce, Chris and Kevin back (my fallen comrades from 'the white school')." The deaths of such amazing guys will always weigh heavily on my mind, and I will never forget them or that they died serving the interests of Canada and its people. The sobering reality, however, is that I can never bring them back and despite my confidence I often find I ask myself questions. Have I lived up to what my accomplishments suggest? Have I been able to learn the lessons I was taught and take the best of everybody in order to be a better man? Have I lived up to the example set by guys like Adam, Johnny, Jamie and Jon Hamilton? Am I the man that was their friend and fellow soldier, the man Ma and grandma raised, the man my mentors inspired and the man that was honoured with the Star of Military Valour and the Vimy Award?

I hope to be able to live up to being the man that General Natynczyk encouraged me to continue to be.

About the Author

Master Warrant Officer (MWO) MacDonald has served in the Canadian Forces as an Infantryman for 21 years and has been deployed operationally overseas five times. He is a recipient of the Star of Military Valour as well as the Vimy Award. MWO MacDonald currently serves as the Company Sergeant Major of Charlie Company in the Third Battalion, Princess Patricia's Canadian Light Infantry.

ACCOMPLISHMENT:
HOW MUCH IS ENOUGH?

AH-HAHS:

TAKE AWAYS:

ACTION ITEM:

Life Lessons From an Ethical Warrior

By Jack E. Hoban

As a young Marine Captain, just off the drill field at the Recruit Depot in San Diego, I decided to earn my Master's Degree at night. It was there that I met my mentor, Robert "Bob" Humphrey; he was one of my professors.

A little background on Humphrey's storybook life is important. Bob Humphrey was a child of the Great Depression. Those were the days when life's lessons were learned in the school of hard knocks and he actually earned money as a semi-professional boxer. He also rode freight trains, worked in the Civilian Conservation Corps (the CCCs) and finally joined the Merchant Marines. He transferred to the U.S. Marine Corps during World War II and became a rifle-platoon leader on Iwo Jima, receiving a gunshot wound that ended his hopes for a professional boxing career. After he was honorably discharged, he earned a Harvard Law degree and settled into teaching economics at MIT. During the Cold War, he went back overseas to see if his worldly experiences and Ivy League education would guide him in solving America's self-defeating "ugly Americanism" and it did. In other words, he was a hell of a man and a real warrior—as opposed to me who just *thought* I was.

I thought I was a tough guy and certainly looked and acted the part well. I would walk around town with a scowl on my face, challenging everyone I met with my eyes. Those of you who have some martial arts training, have you ever fantasized about using it? I did. I would walk into a bar, look around, and then mentally "knock off" everyone in the place before I could relax, sit down and enjoy a beer.

My aggressive attitude started to irritate Humphrey to the point that he finally took me aside and said, "Jack, I have to ask, do you realize that you make people uncomfortable? You seem to be trying to intimidate everyone you meet." I shrugged, but inside I was secretly pleased, as in "Well they *should* be uncomfortable, because I am such a 'badass'!" Humphrey could see that I wasn't getting it. But he was patient and smart. Rather than telling me I was a fool, he gave me some extra homework. He said, "Jack, tonight when you go out, instead of looking at everyone like you want to intimidate them, try this instead: say to yourself 'Everyone in this place is a little *safer* because I am here.'"

I respected Humphrey very much by this time, so I decided to try his suggestion. I often went to a place in Ocean Beach called the Red Garter. It was like the bar in *Star Wars*—full of tough guys (and gals), various military folks, bikers, Soviet spies (this was during the Cold War) and plenty of trouble if you wanted it. But this time, instead of acting like my usual self, I stopped in the doorway, surveyed the scene and said to myself: "Everyone in this place is a little safer because I am here; anyone in need has at least one friend because of me and my skills."

Well everybody ignored me, of course. Nothing happened on the outside, but on the inside—well, even as I write this, I get that tingly feeling on my face and scalp—I had one of those life-changing epiphanies. I realized, "Wow, that feels a *lot* better than what I was doing!" That lesson in context changed my life and maybe even saved it. It turned me from a self-styled "hard case" into a protector and I continue to share this story with my audiences all over the world. Over the years we began to call it the "Warrior Creed," and I invite you to try it yourself tonight:

Wherever I go,

everyone is a little bit safer because I am there.

Wherever I am,

anyone in need has a friend.

When I return home,

everyone is happy I am there.

"It's a better life!"

Another Humphrey story that has impacted me beyond measure is one about his work overseas during the Cold War that has clear implications of importance to this day. We refer to it in our work with the Marines as "The Hunting Story" and it follows as such:

After WWII, America was the undisputed leader of the world. For a while everyone loved us, even our former enemies, but soon people began to resent us due to our perceived superior attitudes. We Americans found this resentment unjustified and ungrateful. In one particular country, the unrest was beginning to have strategic implications during that delicate time of détente. Humphrey's job was to find a solution.

The basic problem was that the Americans working in a poorer, ally country thought that the local people were "smelly, ignorant, violent, dishonest and lazy" and let them know it. No matter what he did, Humphrey couldn't stop the negative talk. As a result, the local people advocated for the Americans to go home.

One day, as a diversion, Humphrey decided to go hunting for wild boar with some people from the American embassy. They borrowed a truck from the motor pool and headed out to the boondocks, stopping at a village to hire some local men to beat the brush and act as guides.

This village was very poor. The huts were made of mud and there was no electricity or running water. The streets were unpaved dirt and the whole village smelled. Flies were everywhere. The men looked surly and wore dirty clothes. The women covered their faces, and the children had runny noses and were dressed in rags.

It wasn't long before one American in the truck said, "This place stinks." Another said, "These people live just like animals." Finally, a young Air Force man said, "Yeah, they got nothin' to live for; they may as well be dead."

What could you say? It seemed true enough.

But just then, an old sergeant in the truck spoke up. He was the quiet type who never said much. In fact, except for his uniform, he kind of reminded you of one of the tough men in the village. He looked at the young airman and said,

"You think they got nothin' to live for, do you? Well, if you are so sure, why don't you just take my knife, jump down off the back of this truck, and go try to kill one of them?"

There was dead silence in the truck. Humphrey was amazed. It was the first time that anyone had said anything that had actually silenced the negative talk about the local people. The sergeant went on to say, "I don't know either why they value their lives so much. Maybe it's those snotty-nosed kids or the women in the pantaloons. But whatever it is, they care about their lives and the lives of their loved ones, same as we Americans do. And if we don't stop talking bad about them, they will kick us out of this country!"

Humphrey asked him what we Americans, with all our wealth, could do to prove our belief in the peasants' equality despite their destitution. The Tennessee sergeant answered easily, "You got to be brave enough to jump off the back of this truck, knee deep in the mud and sheep dung. You got to be brave enough to walk through this village with a smile on your face. And when you see the smelliest, scariest-looking peasant, you got to be able to look him in the face and let him know, just with your eyes, that you know he is a man who hurts like you do, and hopes like you do, and wants for his kids just like we all do. It is that way or we lose."

This story also gives me goose bumps because that was the big question! As a Marine, I fancied myself as a warrior and a protector, but was I brave enough to jump off the back of the truck? Even today, when I walk through the mall or sit in the subway or pass through the scary part of town, I wonder if I am confident and secure enough in my values and skills to project an acknowledgment of human equality into the eyes of everyone I meet. Even people who have behaviors I don't particularly like—perhaps even criminal behaviors—can I separate the *relative* value of their behavior (which may be good, bad or indifferent) from the universal *intrinsic* value of their life and remain the protector? Is *everyone* in my presence safer because I am there?

Bob Humphrey died on July 16, 1997, but his wisdom and deeds live on through the Warrior Creed, The Hunting Story and so many other lessons he taught. When faced with tough choices and adversity, I often ask myself, "Am I that man?"

About the Author

Jack Hoban served as a U.S. Marine Corps officer and is a co-founder and subject matter expert for the Marine Corps Martial Arts Program (MCMAP). He is president of Resolution Group International (www.rgi.co), a conflict resolution company, and is a longtime practitioner of martial arts.

Life Lessons From an Ethical Warrior

Ah-Hahs:

Take Aways:

Action Item:

Reflecting On "The Common Denominator of Success"

By Tom McMahon

I recently read Stephen Covey's *The 7 Habits of Highly Effective People* in which he recommends the essay "The Common Denominator of Success" written by Albert E.N. Gray. It was available online, so I read it immediately and was struck with his simple definition of the common denominator of success. The essay is a written copy of a speech the author gave in 1940 at a life insurance salesmen conference. Gray defines success and then provides a list of four habits that successful people in his line of work have cultivated. Although the essay is not attached, I would highly recommend reading the original, as I will be referring to it throughout.

Gray's definition of success is: "*The common denominator of success—the secret of success of every man who has ever been successful—lies in the fact that he formed the habit of doing things that failures don't like to do.*" Wow. So simple, so logical, and so very true. Gray's definition addresses why success is achieved by so few. More importantly, because it is so general in its scope, its application is universal, regardless of your chosen field of endeavor. Finally, his broad definition of success is not based on education, genetics, circumstance or any other external factor, but instead on habit. Dictionary.com defines habit as: "an acquired behavior pattern regularly followed until it has become almost involuntary." For us, the behavior patterns to be discussed here are conscious, chosen and therefore changeable. So, Gray's definition of success is simple, logical, universal and most importantly, it is entirely attainable because it is based on conscious behavior choices that in turn form our habits. Gray offered the following on habits:

> "Every single qualification for success is acquired through habit. Men form habits and habits form futures. If you do not deliberately form good habits, then unconsciously you will form bad ones. You are the kind of man you are because you have formed the habit of being that kind of man, and the only way you can change is through habit."

The author then outlined the four habits that successful life insurance salesmen cultivate. Although I have no background in insurance or sales, Gray's definition of success and the habits he mentioned got me thinking: what do successful people do in general that others don't do? What is it that failures do instead? What are four habits of successful people in my line of work? I felt compelled to consciously examine my habits so I wouldn't, as Gray warned above, unconsciously form bad habits. I came up with the following "success habits" that I think can be applied to any pursuit whether it be academic, athletic, financial, etc.

1. *Cultivate the habit of overcoming the uncomfortable.* The majority of people don't like to be uncomfortable mentally or physically so they devote a tremendous amount of time to either pursuing pleasure or avoiding discomfort regardless of what their goal is. Most people can relate to this concept and would agree that some or most of their behaviors have been driven by this idea (seeking pleasure and avoiding pain). If this is true, then by Gray's definition, successful people or the minority of people are doing something different; they are cultivating the habit of overcoming the uncomfortable and forsaking the pleasurable. For example, taking the leap of faith in starting your own business, eating better, being uncomfortable in the gym every day, having that difficult conversation with a coworker, or dedicating time to develop a certain physical skill set are all potentially uncomfortable things to do with a seemingly unending supply of distractions and pleasantries in our lives. Successful people would make the conscious choice to forsake the comfortable couch and cultivate the habit of overcoming the uncomfortable. So, our challenge in the quest to cultivate the habit of overcoming the uncomfortable could be to identify three things every day that are nagging at us or are in need of our attention and then overcome the uncomfortable. Have the difficult conversation, make the harder choice to eat responsibly and exercise vigorously, develop a budget and stick to it, or put in the extra time

to better that skill set. You name it. They will be the three things every day that you will work on as you *cultivate the habit of overcoming the uncomfortable.*

2. *Cultivate the habit of goal setting and achieving.* Where are you going and how are you going to get there? Is what you are doing right now getting you closer to your goal? If not, why are you doing it and what do you need to do differently to get there? The easiest way to do this is to continually ask yourself what Brian Willis refers to as "Life's Most Powerful Question" and that is quite simply, "What's important now?" Once you can imagine your goal and be honest with where you are at now, you simply have to close the distance on your goal. We do this by setting and achieving goals while being continually guided by "What's Important Now." It's not enough to say I want to retire wealthy or make the Varsity basketball team. You need a plan to get there because if you don't have a plan, anything will do. And remember what Gray said about habits: if we don't deliberately form good habits, we will unconsciously form bad ones. Your plan has to be a series of small specific goals that will get you from where you are now to your objective within a certain timeline. Once you have committed to your goals, your mission is to achieve them and you will get there by always asking "What's Important Now?" Is what I'm doing right now getting me closer to my ultimate goal? For example, most people drive with maps or GPS units in their vehicles for this reason. They have a goal to get to a certain destination within a set timeline and their GPS keeps them on track toward their final destination. Your smaller goals are your waypoints en route to your final destination: your ultimate goal. Take a moment to celebrate as you reach your waypoints with the knowledge that you will in time arrive at that ultimate goal. So what are your goals? How are you getting there? What's your plan? Name three goals you would like to achieve in a reasonable time frame. Map out how you will get there. Set waypoints

that will lead you to your final goal. Ask yourself, "What's important now?" to keep you on track as you *cultivate the habit of goal setting and achieving.*

3. *Cultivate the habit of lifelong learning and personal growth.* We are either growing as people or not, but we are never staying the same. So, by definition, we should always be evolving or changing to grow or improve as people. If our tomorrow is the same as yesterday, we have not changed; we have not improved. There must be some daily reading, a seminar, a conference or a course, or a daily ritual that makes us better. Therefore, cultivate the habit of directing your personal change and your personal growth. Be the best that you can be by actively directing your growth. In keeping with the other habits, set a goal of no television for three months and use this time that was previously dedicated to TV for reading. Set a goal to read two books a month for these three months or use that newly free time to take an evening walk with your partner, learn a language, take dance lessons, or learn meditation. Make it whatever you want it to be, but use it to grow and change and learn. We must not be the same person tomorrow that we were today or yesterday. We must *cultivate the habit of lifelong learning and personal growth.*

4. *Cultivate the habit of sharing your knowledge, skills and victories.* The knowledge and abilities one has as a "success" should be shared with others. It would be a shame if you had some skill or knowledge that could help another person and it went unshared. Invest in the growth and betterment of others by sharing your skills and knowledge with family, friends and coworkers. Share your knowledge, your skills and your achievements with others to help them become better. Making people better and assisting them in their growth is my definition of leadership and when there's investment in people through sharing knowledge and skills, there is leaving a legacy. You and I will not live forever but our influence

through leadership and positively impacting others will long outlast us. Tell and show others how you have done what you've done and help them with their goals, learning and personal growth. Hopefully they will do the same and your legacy of sharing of knowledge and skills will continue until long after you are gone. What are three things you could share with someone else to leave a legacy or improve things for another? Set your goal and *cultivate the habit of sharing your knowledge, skills and victories.*

I think we all have unique skills, abilities and goals that we must develop to reach our full potential and that this process does not happen by accident. It must be desired, planned for and worked toward. Along this journey of ours, we must share what we have learned with others as part of our own ongoing development. Sharing our successes can only serve to make us and others better, and that should be something we all strive for. I believe all of these objectives may be realized through reflecting on Albert Gray's definition of success and by cultivating the above four habits in our journey of continual betterment.

About the Author

Tom McMahon has been a member of the Calgary Police Service for the last fourteen years and has worked Patrol and the Mountain Bike Team downtown, the Firearms Training Unit, the Uniform Anti Gang Team and has worked for the last three years as a member of the Tactical Team. He has a B.A. from the University of Alberta. He lives in Calgary with his wife Lacey.

Reflecting On "The Common Denominator of Success"

Ah-Hahs:

Take Aways:

Action Item:

Slim

By Ron Kittle

Growing up in a family with six children, you had to learn to listen and to observe. From there, you kind of figured out what was right and what was wrong. But from my perspective, you still had to try something just so you could see why you weren't supposed to do it.

There is no doubt that I was the mischievous one in the family, always pushing everything to the edge. I got plenty of "butt-whooping" to prove it. My listening skills were poor but my eyesight was keen. I absorbed everything. If I saw something done once, I could do it and definitely try to do it better.

I guess it happened one night at home; I was maybe nine or ten years old at the time. My dad came home from work with a broken arm; they had put a cast on him. Up to that point, I didn't think my dad could get hurt. No one said much at dinner and we all just looked at him. I had heard people say my dad was more than just a good worker; they said "Slim" was a tough son of a gun.

As morning came, my dad was sitting at the table cutting the cast off his arm with a steak knife. All he said was that they would not let him work with a cast on his arm and he had children to feed and a ball glove to buy for me. And then he was gone, off to work.

It really felt like I was hit over the head with a hammer. It was over 40 years ago, but to this day, what he did and what he said still plays in my head almost every day. At that point, it was like I instantly grew up. I decided right then that I would never let anything get the best of me. I wanted to be more than just good; I wanted to be the tough one. I wanted to be the one that everyone said was the hardest worker around. It was not his advice but it was seeing my dad's actions that put me onto the path I was headed.

There were so many times growing up I wanted the day to never stop. I wanted to keep doing something all the time, and I pretty much did. I played baseball and it was fun to play with the neighborhood kids. But then I found out my dad really liked baseball and he became the coach. He yelled at us—well more like grunted as he was a man of few words. One time, I think he smiled when we made a big league play. My dad was never one to show too many emotions.

He used to tell the players on the team to pack a lunch. We were going to practice and practice long and hard. It didn't bother me because it was what I liked doing. There was not one time I thought I was better than anyone playing baseball and I didn't really care. But I did care to do the best I could—I wanted to impress my dad.

One game—I might have been fifteen or sixteen—I hit five home runs but I made an error while playing shortstop. The runner was a friend of mine from another school and I was giving him a chance to beat my throw to first base. I threw a bullet to first and handcuffed the first baseman. The runner was safe. For that my dad did not allow me to have dinner that night because I hadn't focused and performed the best I could have. My mom handed me two hot dogs over the shower curtain…the best hot dogs I've ever had.

I was lucky enough to get to work with my dad in the steel mills of Gary, Indiana. It was dirty, smelly, long and hard work. But I got to see what my dad did for a living; a man with a sixth-grade education that read blueprints and ran crews that built buildings. Everybody looked to Slim for answers and they feared him if they messed up. That was the world where my dad worked to feed and support his family—and buy me a ball glove.

The buzz around the mill was Slim's boy was out there working. They heard he was a ball player who might be pretty good. Trust me; there was no way I was getting treated with kid gloves. They had expectations from Slim's kid. I was there to impress them and I was not about to let them down. I had it set in my mind that I would never ever let anyone out-work me, no matter what. And no matter how bad I felt, I had to get it done. The scene played in my head again of my dad cutting off his own cast.

During my first season in major league baseball, I broke my neck. I came home and had very little hope of doing anything. One day my dad came into my room; I was lying there with a steel halo screwed to my head. Slim looked at me and said, "Hey boy, it's time to show the world what you're made of." I didn't need another thing said to me.

My dad passed away in 1994. I was fortunate enough that I got to show him that I worked hard and got to the top of a game he loved; baseball. I wanted to pay him back for the lessons in life he didn't realize he gave me. I bought him a new truck to say "Thank You." I bet there were not ten words said, but I knew he was happy and that was good enough for me. I'm not even sure I ever told him I loved him until two days before he passed away. But he knew it; just a thing between him and me.

Since his passing, I've learned that you never pay someone back, you just pay it forward. I'm glad I get to do that in life. I get to speak publically giving motivational speeches. And I also have two children. I try hard to show them paths they should follow to better themselves and to set examples for years to come. I'm not sure when they will recognize it, or if they have. But if they listen and observe, like everyone, they will see their version of Slim at the kitchen table.

James W. Kittle- Father, and Slim to many

About the Author

Ron Kittle is a former major league baseball player. He played ten seasons; Chicago White Sox (1982-86, 1989, 1991), New York Yankees (1986-87), Cleveland Indians (1988), Baltimore Orioles (1990). He was the 1983 AL Rookie of the Year. Ron is currently the Ambassador for the Chicago White Sox as well as a motivational speaker.

Ron has authored one book, *Ron Kittle's Tales from the White Sox Dugout*. He is working on his second book. Ron's hobbies include woodworking, creating baseball/sports art, and riding his Harley. He is constantly seeking new and innovative ways to market and promote his ideas and projects.

Ron has two children—Hayley 25 and Dylan 23—and a dog named Harley.

Ron Kittle

www.ronkittle.com

219-331-3575

SLIM

AH-HAHS:

TAKE AWAYS:

ACTION ITEM:

Identify two ways you can "Pay it Forward"

The Shattered Mirror

By Spencer Moore

Fathers are notorious for living their lives vicariously through their sons; I was no different. Whether it is sports, academics or social networking, we want our sons to succeed; even more, we want them to surpass our accomplishments.

David Spencer Moore arrived in October 1981. A strapping lad, David was cute as a button and ready to start walking. Born into a law enforcement family, we hoped that he might find other interests in his life. I was a police lieutenant on the Indianapolis Police Department. I retired with 42 years in law enforcement in 2006. David's mother, Jo, would join IPD in 1985, adding to the influence of the police profession. Jo continues her service as a street supervisor.

David was a good kid. He was very bright with a high IQ and a strong body. He excelled in academics and athletics. He also excelled in the social world, becoming very popular with his running buddies and the girls. He was known as someone you could take your problems to.

When it came time for college, David had several full-ride offers based on academics and athletics. His mother and I hoped he would take the four-year scholarship from the Coast Guard Academy (rated as one of the most difficult to earn). David instead chose the full ride NROTC scholarship offered by the Navy at Purdue. Only one thousand of these NROTC scholarships are offered nation-wide annually.

David had expressed several times as he matured his desire to be a Marine Corps officer and in 2000 it seemed his dream was just a few years away. However, fate turned an ugly face. A high school wrestling injury to his knee reappeared. We found that the original repair was improperly completed and just waiting for the opportunity to resurface.

The Corps decided that the injury made David a poor risk due to the physical demands of an USMC officer. David was released from the NROTC program after ardent appeals from the Purdue NROTC Command.

In 2003, David's junior year, he turned his attention to his other dream: becoming a police officer.

In 2004, after graduating from Purdue, David was accepted as an IPD Probationary Officer in Class 102—"Warriors in Blue." He successfully completed the academy and the field-training program and was assigned as a regular officer in 2005.

David's work ethic became a centerpiece of his character; he was selected by the Department as the Rookie of The Year. That honor was followed by his peers selecting him as the Rookie of The Year, announced at the Employee's Recognition Banquet.

David continued to earn awards and recognition for his police work. In late 2009 he was involved in a blazing gun battle with a Mexican drug cartel assassin on the city's west side. Investigation indicated that while on patrol around midnight he heard gunshots and went to the sound. He became embroiled in a gun battle between two drug groups receiving hostile fire from both sides. David used his training and his courage to engage both groups, exchanging numerous shots with the gunmen. The gun battle finally became a confrontation between the cartel assassin and David. David was later awarded the Medal of Valor for his action during a frontal assault on the gunman in which he was able to deliver a fatal volley of shots, ending the gun battle. He was accredited with saving a number of lives that night.

David's career kept expanding with assignments to specialty units. In 2009 David was accepted as member of the Bomb Squad; a position that he relished.

Jo and I were so pleased with our son. It seemed David would one day have an important position within the Indianapolis Metropolitan Police Department (IPD and the Marion County Sheriff Department merged in 2006 to form IMPD).

Sunday, January 23, 2011

I had just returned from church and it was about 9:20 A.M. The phone rang. A good friend of mine asked me a simple question, "Is

David working today?" I knew immediately that something was wrong. Of course he was working that day; it was his second day on Day Shift. My friend, a police officer, told me he thought David had been hurt. Hurt? Then he told me, "I think he's been shot."

What goes through your mind at this time is unbelievable and at such speed it seems unreal. I thought of his childhood dreams, of my dreams of his accomplishments, of future grandchildren (David was not married) and what would I tell his mother.

First things first, I had to contact the Department and find out what's going on. I called the communications center, identified myself and asked if David had been hurt. The answer chilled my very being: "Yes, he's been shot in the head." That was all they knew.

Oh God, this couldn't be happening. Now I was worrying about recovery, the effects of the wounds, what the future would hold and how I would tell his mother.

A few hours earlier I had dropped Jo off at the airport. She was in the air en route to Florida for a vacation cruise with her brother and sister. Now it became more than just how to tell her but what I would tell her.

Around 9:30 A.M. a car arrived to take me to the hospital. We made the drive quickly as it was on Sunday. I arrived at Wishard Hospital to find the area clogged with police cars…never a good sign.

Department friends and the hospital staff met me at the door.

I learned that David had been shot several times during a routine traffic stop. The suspect, still on the loose, but later arrested that day, had opened fire immediately striking David in the leg, in the vest and, the most threatening, twice in the head. It did not look good.

They couldn't tell me much more until they got a good MRI, and that was hard to do because David continually went into cardiac arrest when they moved him. The doctors, who were magnificent, told me that we would have to wait for him to stabilize before being able to really define the overall prognosis.

During this time, friends and the Department officials were doing their best to contact Jo. They also had the additional task of tracking down the shooter, a career criminal. Near one o'clock Jo sent me a text message that she had arrived in Florida. It was then that I made the hardest phone call in my life.

I was honest with her, telling her it did not look good. She was able to get on a non-stop plane back to Indianapolis and arrived at the hospital around 6:00 P.M. David's sister, Carol, arrived shortly afterwards. Other members of the family began collecting at the hospital as well as hundreds of police officers.

Jo and I began discussing all the possibilities. We agreed that David would not want to live in a state that prevented him from being a police officer or at least living a "normal" life.

Mostly we hunkered down for the night and waited, making continual visits to his bedside. David was never alone, not for minute; that was never going to happen.

Monday, January 24, 2011

It was a long day. We had several meetings with the doctors, going over their findings and the prognosis.

Friends flowed into the hospital, his friends and ours. High school friends, teachers, college friends, NROTC buddies, police family members, dignitaries, press, church members and others came to support David and us.

So many stories were exchanged. Actually, we learned a lot of things about David; I'm proud to say they were all good things.

We received notes and cards of well wishing. Many grade school classes throughout the Metro Area sent hand-drawn get well cards. People wrote into the local newspapers extolling contact they had had with David; talking of his professionalism, his compassion and concern. It seemed that David had touched half the population of Indianapolis.

Jo and I talked about how caring he had been, well beyond our knowledge. We also talked about the future. We did not want to let go of the hope that he would recover.

We waited as the night arrived and passed. Tomorrow we would have our answer according to the doctors.

Tuesday, January 25 2011

The day began as usual with hundreds of citizens, offices and friends clogging the hospital hallways. Finally we began to send everyone to an auditorium in the hospital. There were so many well-wishers that it was impossible to keep track.

The press, of course, was out in full force. I give them credit for being respectfully and displaying true concern. In the afternoon, we had a conference with the doctors and got our answer. It was not what we wanted to hear, but realistically expected.

David would not recover. His wounds were too severe and his brain had suffered extensive damage, far beyond their capability to fix.

Now it was time to consider David's legacy. With our hearts still hurting from the news, Jo and I decided that David would be an organ donor. We would meet with the donor group later that evening, but now it was time to tell David's friends and his community that we were going to give him back to God.

With tears and aching hearts, we first met with the police family. As it was to us, the news was devastating to many.

Next we faced the press and announced that David would not recover. The subsequent out-pouring from the community was unbelievable. Often it was as if they had lost a son. We were gathered into their arms and held lovingly.

Wednesday, January 26, 2011

During the night, the hospital staff arranged David in his bed so that his mother could spend this last night with him. It was an act that we treasure with the greatest of appreciation.

At around 4:00 A.M. that morning, Jo begins to notice that David's monitors were showing he was failing quickly.

At 6:18 A.M. David passed into God's hands.

We announced David's passing to our police family.

Then came the news conference where we announced his death and the organ donor program. We held strongly to a theme we established early on: "Celebrating the Life of A Warrior."

Around 4:00 P.M. we left the hospital, admittedly with great reluctance. Jo put it best, "We now must get used to the new normal, a life without our son."

The next few days were extremely busy. The weather was horrible. A major ice storm hit the city making a full honors ceremony impossible. Regardless, what was accomplished was splendid. The local NBA venue, Conseco, was offered as a site for David's funeral and we gladly accepted their generous offer.

The world outside Conseco was a miserable winter scene. Ice was so bad that it was nearly impossible to use the roadways, yet thousands showed up for David's funeral. The pomp and circumstance was perfectly executed.

The irony of the weather was that most businesses and all schools were closed throughout Indiana. Therefore, many families got to view the ceremony on television or online streaming. We received numerous cards for families expressing their awe and appreciation for being able to watch the ceremony in its entirety. Among those expressions were cards from all over the world. It was just mind-boggling.

Due to the weather we delayed David's internment until February 4. It was a private ceremony with just the family, a few friends and coworkers in attendance.

We walked away with tears in hearts and eyes. The finality of David's death was burdensome, almost too much so.

The Legacy

Immediately, however, we began thinking of his legacy. We formed a not-for-profit foundation, instituted several scholarships at college and high school level and were humbled by the community's love. For the first time in our city's history a street was named in honor of a fallen officer. We began the process to reach out to the recipients of his organs.

The latter experience has become so meaningful. Jo and I are in constant contact with recipients and are enjoying establishing a strong, meaningful friendship with a couple of them.

The Shards

Speaking strictly from the standpoint of a father, the shattered mirror destroyed the reflection of David. It did not take away the past, but it ended the future for many hopes and plans.

There was no longer the hope of grandchildren, the direct continuance of the line.

I can remember our travels, just he and I. I always felt safe in his presence. David's absence now leaves large, gaping holes in that mental security.

Jo and I had hopes of seeing David rise in the ranks through the Department to a position of authority where he would establish himself as a trustworthy leader. It is little solace that he is remembered clearly as one of the finest officers the Department produced.

But, I think most importantly, there is the absence of future security for his mother. I always felt that when my time came—I am several years older than Jo—David would be here to make sure his Mom was safe, secure and taken care of. That's gone. I now worry about that lack of care for Jo. That's not to say our daughter cannot fill the void, but I always looked at that as a primary duty for David.

We, parents, are certainly not built to follow our children in death. It is unnatural. It is a burden beyond description. It is the shard that cuts to the quick.

Faith in God is the only cure; it is what makes life continue to be worth living. But as for me, David's death has taken all the fear out of dying. I know he awaits me and I look forward to the day when once again I can feel his embrace and know that I am home safe.

Editor's Note by Brian Willis:

I did not know David Moore when he was alive. Since his death I have come to know David through Spencer and Jo and through the men and women of the IMPD who continue to honor David's legacy. Some of you reading this book knew David, most will not. You have, however, known someone like David; an amazing young man, a warrior who gave his life in sacrifice to his community or country. When we lose the David Moore's of the world you need to stop and ask yourself "Am I that man?" Am I that man that David modeled for me? Am I that man that David would have been proud to call a fellow warrior, a friend, a fellow Crossfitter, or a mentor? David and other heroes and warriors like him set a powerful example for all of us based on how they lived their lives. They live life with passion, with honor, with integrity, with commitment to a worthy cause and with unconditional love. Seek out the David Moore's of the world while they are alive and learn from them, model them and seek to become like them.

About the Author

Spencer L. Moore retired from the Indianapolis Police Department in 2006 after 42 years serving as a police officer. Spencer continues to live in Indianapolis with Jo Ann, his wife of 37 years. Jo joined the Indianapolis Police Department in 1985 and continues to serve as a street supervisor. They have two children, Carol and David. David is deceased. He died from gunshot wounds received in the line of duty as a member of the Indianapolis Metropolitan Police Department in January 2011. Carol is a schoolteacher in the Indianapolis area and has two children. Spencer is a veteran of the Vietnam conflict. He serves as the chairman of The Officer David S. Moore Foundation, a not-for-profit foundation that supports civic projects.

THE SHATTERED MIRROR

AH-HAHS:

TAKE AWAYS:

ACTION ITEM:

What does it mean to you to "Be a Man"?

Celebrating the Life of a Warrior

Bill Westfall

Officer David Moore most likely never suspected that 60-year-old Thomas Hardy had murder in his heart as he climbed from the stolen vehicle he was driving in Indianapolis on that cold, overcast Sunday morning in January 2011. David Moore was too good of a police officer. If he'd had the slightest hint of Hardy's intent he would have been able to defend himself. A stellar athlete, he was captain of an undefeated state championship high school football team, described over and over as a young man who possessed a strength and wisdom well beyond his years. This 2005 IMPD Rookie of the Year was the epitome of the officer one hopes to hire, retain and at some point partner with. He was the officer you wanted in your neighborhood as a community member. He was that good of an officer and that good of a man.

What happened next happened so quickly that David never knew of Hardy's intent until it was too late. Shot four times, twice in the head, once in the chest and once in the thigh. It was the head wounds that ultimately lead to David's death three days later.

As Hardy sped from the scene and David lay on the cold ground with his life ebbing from his limbs. Jo Ann Moore, David's mother and a sergeant with the Indianapolis Metropolitan Police Department, would shortly be landing at Miami International Airport anticipating a vacation with her sister and brother. David's father, Spencer Moore—a much respected, retired lieutenant of nearly forty years' service with Indianapolis Police Department—was enjoying a leisurely morning at home after having dropped his wife at the airport and attending an early church service.

I heard about the shooting of David Moore from friends with IMPD. I happened to be in California completing a training session when Sgt. Rick Snyder called and advised me of the shooting and reminded me that I had met Jo Ann Moore when she had attended IMPD's Leadership Institute, a four week school in which we have taught since its inception. Rick indicated to me that Jo Ann had asked about the possibility of me speaking on her behalf at David's funeral that they anticipated would be the following week. Rick also suggested that I search the internet to stay current on the events as they unfolded.

My first introduction to Spencer Moore was through a video I viewed online that had been posted by the Indianapolis media of the announcement of David's shooting. I recalled Jo Ann Moore immediately. You just don't forget Jo Ann Moore once you have met her. She is outgoing, expressive, full of love of life and family, and any conversation you have with her will be recalled simply because of the sincerity of those traits.

My last conversation with her followed that final session of a three-day block that we provide during the Institute. It is at the conclusion that we provide each participant with a challenge coin. The coins contain two quotes, one from an uncle of mine who was an Indiana judge who told me at age twenty-four when I entered law enforcement, "Good for you, young man. If you do that job properly there is nothing more noble you will do with your life." The second quote contains a leadership test about doing the right thing, at the right time, in the right way and for the right reason. Jo Ann had received her coin and had left and then returned and told me about her son David whom she hoped would soon attend The Leadership Institute. She asked, "Would you have another coin that I could possibly give to David?" She knew he would appreciate what the coin represented. You don't forget such conversations. So my memory was fresh of Jo Ann, but I knew nothing of Spencer Moore.

Spencer Moore was in his late sixties, and yet as I looked into the face of this grieving father, I would not have believed him to be that age. There is a bit of boyishness in Spencer's face that reveals his personality and belies his age.

Spencer Moore has a distinct voice, a voice I believe that any aspiring media type would crave. It's not just the voice but also his content, coupled with a forthrightness and conviction, sincerity and intelligence that so often are missing in public statement. Spencer began the press conference, "We will celebrate the life of a warrior and not grieve the loss of a son." And with those words Spencer Moore set the tone for his family, the media and his community. There was no anger in his voice, no comments of retribution or vengeance. There was only a sense of sadness with a resolute determination that this loss would be done with dignity and grace. And with that statement began the path of these two remarkable public servants to console a grieving family, a grieving brotherhood and sisterhood of officers, and a community—once introduced to David and his parents—who would grieve with them.

Over the next few days I watched interview after interview with the Moore's and each time the calm, distinct, articulate and intelligent voice of Spencer Moore resonated to provide information about David's day-to-day condition. But within three long sleepless days, hope progressed to the harshness of reality and the obvious became acceptance; this chapter of David's young life would come to an end. Recognizing the futility, the family announced that David was being kept alive only through artificial means but with purpose. And that purpose would be to provide life and hope to a number of patients and family awaiting organ donations. And then on January 26, 2011 Spencer Moore announced to the Indianapolis community and to a vigilant police community that David Moore had passed.

After being notified of his mother's request, I made immediate arrangements to fly to Indianapolis and the following morning met with Jo Ann and Spencer Moore. As I entered the home there was a sense of seriousness about the moment, but overwhelming the seriousness was a pervasive sense of joy and celebration. At the center of that energy were Spencer and Jo Ann. Spencer put my wife and me at ease with his ever-present wit and humor that was not feigned or in any way strained. It was who he was and I could see that in some way this would be this patriarch's finest hour.

Jo Ann explained that she did not feel comfortable addressing such a large crowd under the circumstances and asked if I would speak on her behalf. There were three things that were important to her. The first was to define her son as a true warrior, removing the sting of the word warrior as it applied to that of a peacekeeper by using words that would reflect both steel and velvet. She wanted me to describe how David had both the strength and courage to do his duty but also had compassion and sensitivity in all his relationships. Secondly, she asked that I speak to David's legacy. Thirdly, given that Spencer had survived a terrible accident with minor injuries while on a COPS charity bicycle ride that took the lives of two officers participating in the ride, that I recognize the suffering of survivors, the wounded warrior. She went on to explain with great emphasis that the outpouring of grief and condolences to them was overwhelming, reassuring and heartwarming but she knew how many of David's family, friends and co-workers could so easily be lost in this moment and to somehow reassure them that they should commit to taking care of each other.

It became resoundingly clear to me that in this most horrific moment of loss, these two remarkable people had put aside their needs and were focused on all those in their home, their community and their police department. I was taken aback. No parent is bequeathed a gene to deal with the loss of a child in their lifetime. From the moment this notification tore through their hearts, theirs was not a message of retribution but a message of celebration of the life and dedication of their son. They set a tone of response so the community could begin the healing process. Spencer had set that tone with the words, "This would be the celebration of life not the grieving of a loss of a son."

From that Sunday until the following Tuesday I have never worked harder on a presentation in the many years that I have stood before a podium. The morning of the funeral ushered in one of the worst ice storms that Indianapolis has ever experienced. Three-inch layers of ice blanketed streets and trees across the city but somehow the police community and the community aroused themselves and went about its duty to bury its guardian son.

The service had to be held at the Conseco Fieldhouse Arena for literally the thousands that would attend even under such awful weather conditions. The presentations made that morning as part of the eulogy were heartwarming and at the same time heart rendering. Classmates and friends spoke, revealing and sharing stories of David's life that were peppered with humor. It intensified the realization of such a terrible loss to family, community and even humankind. David was that big of a personality.

Then it was Spencer Moore's turn. I tried to imagine how a father provides a eulogy for a child, especially a child lost in such a needless manner. For all that was troubling Thomas Hardy that morning, most likely one of the most sympathetic would have been David Moore. Spencer Moore's voice was resolute, calming and reassuring and his words were that of celebration and grace. And not once, not once did his voice break. I followed Spencer Moore and as I walked to the podium I was asking myself, "How does one follow such a eulogy given with such sincerity, humility, decency and poise?" Very simply…you can't. I played Everett to Spencer's Lincoln. The Moore family did not need me. Jo Ann did not need me to speak on behalf of her family. She had her hero, she had her spokesman and rightly so.

As I left the ceremony, exiting with the Moore family, there was a thin blue line of officers arranged to pay tribute to David and his family. I looked into their faces, their lips literally turning blue and trembling from the conditions they had endured while waiting in the January cold. It was apparent to me that we could have saved them a great deal of suffering had Spencer simply spoken to us about his son.

Thomas Hardy was sentenced to life without parole on April 5, 2012. At his hearing family, friends and co-workers were allowed to speak. Each had a part. Each had an important message for Hardy to hear. In typical humility, when it was Spencer's turn he simply used the words of one of David's fellow officers to speak on his behalf; a letter Spencer had received that very morning. It was a message that David's example in life and in his death made him want to be a better man and a better officer.

And then it was Jo Ann Moore's turn. She was eloquent, sincere, heartfelt, and somehow she found the strength to extend compassion to Hardy. In the aftermath of the hearing, Spencer diverted constant attention to his wife to a waiting media.

As I reflect on the memories of this past year and the many stories that so richly illustrated Spencer's life and accomplishments and ask, "Am I that man?" The answer is resoundingly, "No!" Most likely I will never be. For Spencer Moore is much like Browning's quote, "A man's reach should exceed his grasp, else what is a Heaven for?" He is the reach that exceeds our grasp, but in our attempt he has made so many, not just me, better for the effort.

And now it is so obvious why David was such a remarkable young man. That seed did not fall far from that tree. God bless you, Spencer and Jo Ann Moore and I thank you for piloting all of us—your family, your friends, your fellow officers and your community—through this path of grace, humility, compassion and courage. For all this tragedy has wrought each of us, because of you both, we have been most richly blessed.

About the Author

Bill Westfall began his law enforcement career with the Alaska State Troopers in 1968 and has served with the Florida Department of Law Enforcement, taking an early retirement as a deputy director when assuming the director's position of the Montana Law Enforcement Academy in 1986. He has focused his study and taught and continues to teach in the law enforcement leadership arena for more 25 years. Bill is a former Marine and Vietnam Veteran and sincerely believes that "if you do this work properly there is nothing more noble you will do with your life."

CELEBRATING THE LIFE OF A WARRIOR

AH-HAHS:

TAKE AWAYS:

ACTION ITEM:

What changes have you made in your
life as a result of reading this book?

What additional changes do you need
to make?

Sport at its Best

By Duff Gibson

I believe we spend a lot of time worrying about whether or not the celebrities and sports heroes our children watch on television are good role models. The reality is that more often than not our children model their behavior after people they see every day, most likely a parent, a teacher or a coach. A friend of mine named Bob, who happens to be in his seventies now, told me of an incident that happened when he was in high school and the impact it has had on him throughout his life:

> "There was a football match being played against our archrival. Well, have you heard of the old "sleeper play" where you take three players off the field and send back two into the huddle hoping the opposition doesn't notice the missing player crouched down near the sideline pretending to be part of the crowd? Well this is what our team did and it looked like the trick was going to work, when out of the crowd near the crouching lad came this bustling old man, dressed in his suit and black teaching gown and wielding his cane high above his head. He gave the lad a couple of good licks with the cane while yelling in his booming voice, "We don't play like this at Ridley, we don't play like this at Ridley!" It was the dreaded headmaster. Well whether we won the game or not I cannot recall, but the lesson of play the game fairly and properly was reinforced and has lasted me a lifetime."

There are undoubtedly those who would argue that the old sleeper play isn't breaking any rules and getting caught by it is a valuable lesson in its own right. Times have certainly changed since Bob attended high school. Hitting a kid with a cane is outdated but good teaching practices are not. In my opinion, it takes great courage to interrupt a football game to make a point about fair play and about actually earning what you achieve. It's a great lesson that has served Bob, and I'd imagine the vast majority of his teammates, close to sixty years now.

In my own case, I'd have to say my father had the greatest impact upon the man I am today but there were certainly others that played a role. One of those people was Mr. Little. Mr. Little was a teacher and volleyball coach at Bridlewood Junior Public School in Scarborough when I was a student there in the late 1970s. One of the coolest things (and there isn't a more apt word) about Mr. Little was that he was a volleyball referee at the 1976 Olympics in Montreal!

Montreal was my first exposure to the Olympics and it immediately had a powerful effect on me. To this day I can clearly remember watching many of the events, including Nadia Comaneci getting her perfect 10s in gymnastics and Bruce Jenner winning the decathlon. I can also remember the high jump in which fellow Canadian Greg Joy won a silver medal behind Jacek Wszola of Poland but ahead of the heavily favored Dwight Stones of the United States. Watching those and many other events, I knew somehow I wanted to be a part of it. I didn't even care what sport it would be in—they were all great.

I'm sure you can imagine what it was like for us on the volleyball team having a coach that had actually refereed at the Olympics. It was pretty special. During one particular practice we were arguing as to whether a ball was in or out when Mr. Little called us over and told us about a match at the Olympics in which he had been a backup referee sitting at the official's table immediately adjacent to the court.

As the story goes, there was a rally that ended when one team spiked the ball toward the opposing team's baseline. Although very close to the line, the ball was out but was incorrectly called in by the line judge. The player that hit the ball actually went to the referee and explained that he had hit the ball out and that the call should be reversed. At which point a player on the opposing team, having overheard this, stepped forward and stated that he had touched the ball on the way out and that therefore the call was correct. I don't know if Mr. Little actually said it or not but his inference was that the player who claimed to have touched the ball hadn't. I don't believe Mr. Little specifically stated which teams were involved, but I understood that they were elite teams of the competition who were vying for medals.

I don't remember how we did as a team that year or even if we won a single game, but I remember that story. Being so enthralled by the Olympics and hearing a first-hand account from someone who was not just there, but an integral part of it, was extremely impactful to me. I remember thinking at the time, "This must be how Olympians act," and I still feel the story is an illustration of sport at its absolute best.

The athletes Mr. Little talked about clearly had a great deal of respect for the game, the officials, their opponents and the process. And it's also a great expression of the value they placed on the relationship between how hard you work for something and your own personal satisfaction. On their respective journeys to the medal podium, neither wanted to accept a single point that wasn't earned.

This story remains an inspiration for me, and in my athletic career (and life) I have tried to follow the example as described to us by Mr. Little. My belief is that it was no coincidence that the athletes in his story were on great teams vying for medals at the Olympic Games. Attitude and success go hand in hand. Thank you, Mr. Little, I agree.

About the Author

Duff Gibson lives with his wife and two boys in Calgary, Alberta, Canada. He has a bachelor's degree in Phys Ed from the University of Western Ontario and a Master's degree in Kinesiology from the University of Calgary. As an athlete, Duff competed in many sports including wrestling, rowing, speed skating and bobsleigh before finding skeleton. Career highlights include a World Championship gold medal in 2004, a World Championship bronze medal in 2005 and an Olympic gold medal in 2006 in Torino, Italy. In 2006, Duff was also named Canadian male athlete of the year. In Whistler, Duff helped provide analysis for the skeleton event as part of CTV's 2010 Olympic coverage and as of spring 2010, was named head coach of the Canadian National Skeleton Team. Duff is also a proud member of the Calgary Fire Department at the rank of Senior Firefighter. To read more from Duff Gibson, go to www.SportAtItsBest.com.

Sport at its Best

Ah-Hahs:

Take Aways:

Action Item:

Welcome to the Jungle

By Ron Wallace

There is not just one type of leadership…leading is a function of the mission and the types of followers assigned. Would the same type of leadership work for a group of accountants as it would for a football team? Probably not, but regardless, you are still leading human beings with real lives, ambitions, goals, talents, and insecurities.

Leadership is defined in many ways. The military states: "Leadership is the ability to actively influence others in order to achieve a common goal." A private company may challenge their leaders in a different way.

You need to ask yourself, "Do you want to make decisions that: causes loyalty of your employees to follow your lead; support you when others criticize you; safely tell you when they think you are going down the wrong track; will ensure your workers will accept your value system?"

You may have just been promoted into the ranks of management or maybe moved up the ladder. The kind of leader you will be is up to you. It is yours to do it right…or screw it up. You will have to prove yourself every minute of every day. **You** now play a new role, and if **you** are in an organization that is worth its salt, **you** have to produce.

Did I say you? What I meant is you had better learn how to lead, because it is the people under you who will do the producing. They can make or break you. A leader is defined as someone who gets things done through others. The people who work for a leader should want to perform for that leader. They will walk through fire for their leader and have strong desires to be recognized by him or her for a job well done. It is reported that Napoleon once said that men will work for money, but they'll die for a medal. Recognition is very important for a leader to embrace. A job well done should be acknowledged and rewarded publicly.

Once you step across the line and become a part of the management team, you take on a different role. In your new playbook you have a much different responsibility. This may be the number one play you need to learn and learn quickly. "I am responsible for…" means "I have accepted an assignment to accomplish an objective or to cause it to be accomplished." The job I do will be measured by the results attained, not by expenditure of time and effort or by the completion of certain courses of action. I am willing to be judged by my success or failure in reaching the objective. Always remember, results trump behavior.

No magic bullet can make you a leader. You won't become a better leader by learning from one source. A leader takes the best that they personally experience over a lifetime and adapts those experiences to develop their own style. Great leaders continue to grow and become better leaders their entire life. Leadership is a journey of continual learning, not a destination we one day arrive at.

If there were a magic bullet, it would be to master people skills. It is easy to be a boss. You have the title, the rank, and the inherent right to order others to get things done. Most failed managers were bosses who never figured out the difference between a boss and a leader. They did not learn how to get the most out of their people. Being a tyrant, or unreasonably demanding, does little to motivate others to love working for you and, hence, will usually affect their job performance in a negative manner.

I have learned from some of the best "people" people in the world. I may be able to offer a few approaches to leadership because I have the advantage of hands-on experience and learning from others during my career. I may be one of a handful of people who have seen how managers from companies around the world operate and what they have done right, as well as what they have done wrong. I have worked with the great ones, the marginal ones, and ones that have failed. I much prefer being around the great ones.

I have had thousands of managers at all levels under my direction. I spent 37 of the best years of my life at UPS, retiring as President of UPS International and was one of ten members of the management committee that oversaw more than 400,000 people in a $92 billion worldwide company. I was responsible for UPS operations in nearly 200 countries and served as chairman or co-chairman of 33 boards of directors around the world.

In retirement, I serve as a director on five boards and several foundations. For the past nine years, I have been a reserve Captain in a local police department with twenty-five officers reporting to me. I have run local political campaigns and was chairman of the governor's commission to create an entire new city that included a police and fire department.

Let me reflect on what I believe makes a good leader and offer some simple suggestions you may want to consider; use them if they fit your style. There is no one best way, but many wrong ways can bring the best-intentioned leader to the brink of failure.

Space does not allow me to cover all the leadership lessons I have learned along the way or to go into depth on the lessons I am covering here. If you want to read more, I am writing a book on leadership that will be available later this year. In it I will cover many more leadership skills in greater detail.

Following are three key leadership skills that I think are extremely important:

1. **Mastering people skills.**

   It is the single best trait a leader can have. If you are a people person, you are already on third base. Hopefully you have worked for a leader about whom you've said, "I'd follow him to hell and back...because I know he will get me back." A leader like that, who takes care of his people, is well on the way to long-term success.

   Mastering people skills has many different parts. First, **surround yourself with great people** and make your team strong. Train them, trust them, and turn them loose to do their jobs. With strong people, you don't have to micromanage and get buried in the details. They will do that while you move on to other important things, one being to protect them from unnecessary "busy" work that flows down from above. Learn to delegate, keep score, and hold yourself and others accountable.

Second, **give genuine praise**. Go find the positives, the good things—and talk about them every day. Don't beat the negatives to death. Focus on the positives, "catch" people doing things correctly and acknowledge them for it. If you say good things about someone, that person will follow you to the end of the earth.

2. Know your job.

Learn it from the ground up, know it inside out, and don't be afraid to get your hands dirty. Better yet, know the jobs of your employees. They will respect you for it. I attribute much of my success at UPS to the fact that I started out doing the job that our company is identified with—driving a truck and delivering packages. That experience, and knowing that job and all that goes with it, gave me the credibility that put me light years ahead of those without that level of grass roots experience within our company.

Out work everyone else. That may mean work smarter, not harder, but if it takes more hours then so be it. Learn how to prioritize and stay the course. Know what is important today, tomorrow, and in the future. Good leaders must first be good planners—part of the work-smarter-not-harder formula.

Don't be a yes man, an empty suit. If you feel strongly about something, speak up. Your input is important, that's why you are there. Staff meetings take many turns. You may not get your way and it's okay to agree to disagree but know that once a decision is made, you become an owner of it. You now have an obligation to support it. Never let your people know that you don't agree with the directive.

Know what is on the horizon and plan for it. Don't wait. That makes you—and maybe only you—ready when the time comes. If next year "homeland security" is going to be the hot thing, read about it, get in classes now. Become the local specialist.

Never underestimate yourself. Take calculated risks and go for it. It is okay and strongly recommended to bounce your ideas off others, especially successful players. Be a smart risk taker—don't be among those timid souls who are afraid to go out on a limb. On the other hand, don't shoot from the hip without thinking things through—it's all part of knowing your job.

3. **Be a problem solver, not a problem reporter.**

You are paid to solve problems, not just report them. Never go to someone with a problem until you have worked through it and have some possible solutions. This is another good time to get advice from others. Never go to your boss and dump a problem in his or her lap without being able to offer solutions. If you can't do that, they don't need you. Do your homework and know the details before you talk with superiors.

One of my favorite stories was given to me early in my career. I copied it and freely handed it out to others in the hope that they, too, would understand the importance of getting their act together. Just winging it will put you in quicksand every time. You may have heard it before, but it is a story of two people trying to get a key promotion at a lumber company.

The Hines Story:

The owner of Hines Lumber Company had to fill a top position. Two of his managers were considered, each with equal experience. The choice went to the man with fewer years with the company. Upon learning of the promotion, the other man asked Mr. Hines why he wasn't the one selected. Instead of answering him, Mr. Hines asked him if any lumber had come in that day. The man said he would check, and a few minutes later reported that a carload had arrived. Mr. Hines then wanted to know the type of lumber. After again checking, the manager told him it was #6 pine. Mr. Hines then asked the man how many board feet were in the order. Again leaving to check, he returned shortly with the answer of 3,500 board feet. This type of questioning went on for several minutes; then Mr. Hines asked the man to go into the next room, leaving the door ajar so he could hear.

Mr. Hines then called in the manager who had been promoted and asked him if any lumber had arrived that day. The manager said he would check, and in a few minutes he returned with the following answer, "A carload of #6 pine came in on track three at 9:30 A.M., totaling 3,500 board feet. The lumber was unloaded by 2:00 P.M. and stored in warehouse #18. It was order number 65-03 for the Williams Company, and its value was $16,352.00."

Mr. Hines thanked the man and said he could go. After the second man left, he called in the first manager, who had heard the entire conversation. The first manager said he now understood why the other man had been promoted. GET THE COMPLETE PICTURE THE FIRST TIME.

The list goes on…There are many more lessons I've learned, some big, some small—but all have shaped the success I have had. Hopefully the above ideas help you as well.

About the Author

Ron Wallace was President of UPS International. He was responsible for over 200 countries and territories with over 60,000 people under his direction. He served on the corporate management committee that oversaw the day-to-day operations of UPS which was a 92 billion dollar company with over 400,000 employees. Before retiring he was a director on 33 different boards. He was a member of various trade organizations throughout the world.

Top Ten Fun Facts About Ron Wallace

1. Played semi-pro football for two years in Europe
2. Campaign consultant
3. Presently serves on five boards in the US and one in China
4. Director on two foundations, both of which he was a founding member

5. Captain at Alpharetta Police Department

6. Chairman of the Governors Commission to establish the City of Milton which included starting a fire and police department

7. Chairman of the Charter Commission for the City of Milton

8. Developer

9. Antique Dealer

10. Day Trader

WELCOME TO THE JUNGLE

AH-HAHS:

TAKE AWAYS:

ACTION ITEM:

My Heroes were my Bosses

By Lt. Col. Dave Grossman

As I look back across the years, my heroes were usually my bosses.

First, there's my dad. For many of us our father is our hero. We learn eventually that he is human and therefore flawed. We may rebel in our teen years, but we look back at him as a mentor and hero and, quite rightfully, we honor our fathers. And that is really a great model to use in the relationship we have with our bosses.

As we become fathers ourselves we realize how very flawed we are, how unworthy we are of our children's blind faith and trust, and yet how very much we cherish our children's love. Again, this is not a bad model to keep in mind as we work with our bosses. Let me try to explain.

As a young, 18-year-old punk, a paratrooper and private in the 82nd Airborne Division in 1975, I remember First Sergeant Wingrove. I worked for him as the orderly (selected from a line platoon for who knows what reason) and he was far from gentle. A true gruff old sergeant, but worthy of respect and willing to take care of "his" people.

So many of those leaders in that era were Vietnam vets, and in my eyes, their combat experience immediately gave them credibility. As the years went by, I learned that First Sergeant Wingrove was a veteran of the Special Forces raid to free our POWs late in that war, a real hero even among the spec ops community. I also learned an important lesson: that my bosses had experiences and skills that I couldn't even begin to comprehend. I wanted to learn from them, I wanted to support them and I took great pleasure in working as a member of their team.

As warriors, the experiences of our superiors (even if it is not gunfight-level combat experience) should automatically earn our respect.

Lieutenant Greg Parlier, a West Point grad with a real heart for "mentoring" a young private (although we didn't use that word back then) was also my boss during this time. And to this day he is still a friend. I moved up to be the battalion training NCO, where he was my boss, and I saw even more Vietnam vet NCOs to learn from and respect.

As a young officer, my company commanders were my heroes: Captain Rick Crosby and Captain Ivan Middlemiss. These were good men doing hard jobs and they were always ready to appreciate loyalty and hard work. In truth, they were only a handful of years older than me, but their years of experience added up to a lot. It was easy to respect them, and respect turned into friendship that in some cases continues to this day.

They almost always knew more than me and had things to teach me. I respected their experience and sought their guidance and wisdom. My "mentors" at nearly every stage of my career were my bosses, and that was a positive and rewarding experience.

This kept happening throughout my career. Sure, there were a few stinkers, but it's not even worth it to mention their titles. The military teaches you to say "Roger, out," and drive on, looking for someone you *could* trust and respect. These are the people that deserve my and your attention.

As a leader myself, I always deeply appreciated it when I found loyalty and support in my subordinates. I tried to be a boss that was worthy of the same relationship I had with my bosses. In my eyes, I seldom came up to the standards of those I served under, but I did my best and they were models to emulate, standards to strive for.

As a leader, I began to understand the intense insecurity that those in charge experience. One of the many paradoxes of leadership is if you can admit to yourself that you are insecure then you are more secure than the others. The trick is you can't let your subordinates know that you feel insecure! You must try to communicate confidence... and a degree of confidence *will* come with time.

If you understand your own insecurity—and every human being is insecure—then you begin to understand how very much your bosses crave and need (and deserve) your respect and support. I was fiercely loyal to my bosses.

One final and important point. A good working dog, a "canine partner," expects to be disciplined. A thump or two and it's over: we're back to being partners with a job to do. But if you are screaming and berating, beyond just a snap and a thump, *especially within earshot of others*, then the whipped, humiliated dog has trouble forgetting.

Never forget: "Praise in pubic, punish in private." And if you must punish, make it short, sharp and then be done with it.

We are all human. We have all lost our temper, and most of us in a moment of weakness may have been screaming and berating. But take my advice and *try very hard not to do it.* Teach yourself not to do it. Warriors don't respect leaders who lose their temper. A pilot, a sniper, a bomb technician, or a surgeon must operate *constantly* in "condition yellow." They must never blow their cool. If they leave "condition yellow" they lose fine-motor control and they, or others, can die as a result. The same is true for leaders and especially for warrior leaders. They must *strive* to live in condition yellow.

We are all human. A sharp, short, angry correction under stress is something that happens, although we should try to keep that to a minimum. But as we walk the warrior-leader path, we will be tempted to "experiment" with throwing a hissy-fit because we're in charge, and we can get away with it! And, too often we may think that is the "right" thing to do because that is what *we* have experienced. We never liked it, but it can become ingrained in our behavior and end up coming through us as leaders without our recognition. It's a cycle of bad behavior, much like abused children who end up repeating the pain on their own children.

You may tell yourself that it is only an act, but we are what we train ourselves to be and you are training yourself to lose your temper. We strive for a state of warrior perfection (understanding that we will never achieve perfection), in which we are good subordinates and worthy bosses, and we never lose our temper.

Every day take one more step down the warrior path. And pray that a lifetime of preparation will be sufficient that, at the moment of truth, you will be the wise old warrior-leader who will lead the others home.

About the Author

LT. COL. DAVE GROSSMAN, U.S. Army (Ret.)

Director, Killology Research Group

www.killology.com

Lt. Col. Dave Grossman is a former West Point psychology professor, Professor of Military Science, and an Army Ranger who is the author of *On Combat* (which was nominated for a Pulitzer Prize), *On Killing* (with Loren Christensen), and *Stop Teaching Our Kids to Kill* (with Gloria DeGaetano). President Clinton cited Col. Grossman's research in a national address after the Littleton, Colorado school shootings, and he has testified before the U.S. Senate, the U.S. Congress, and numerous state legislatures. He has served as an expert witness and consultant in state and Federal courts, to include UNITED STATES vs. TIMOTHY MCVEIGH. He helped train mental health professionals after the Jonesboro school shootings, and he was also involved in counseling or court cases in the aftermath of the Paducah, Springfield, and Littleton school shootings. He has been called upon to write the entry on "Aggression and Violence" in the *Oxford Companion to American Military History*, three entries in the Academic Press *Encyclopedia of Violence, Peace and Conflict* and has presented papers before the national conventions of the American Medical Association, the American Psychiatric Association, the American Psychological Association, and the American Academy of Pediatrics. His research has been cited by the President of the United States. Today he is the director of the Killology Research

Group (www.killology.com), and in the wake of the 9/11 terrorist attacks he is has written and spoken extensively on the terrorist threat, with articles published in the *Harvard Journal of Law and Civil Policy* and many leading law enforcement journals, and he has been on the road almost 300 days a year, training elite military and law enforcement organizations worldwide about the reality of combat.

MY HEROES WERE MY BOSSES

AH-HAHS:

TAKE AWAYS:

ACTION ITEM:

Learning, Living, and Leading

By Richard W. "Rick" Myers

Looking back on a 35-year career in policing, what I consider among the most noble of professions, and having served as a leader for 27 years, I have been influenced and mentored by many. There are great role models who surround us, *if* we take the time to look for those behaviors that distinguish their greatness. However, some of the greatest lessons learned have been through self-reflection, which remains among the most critical of leadership traits.

While some successful people have overcome poor family backgrounds, I'm one of the fortunate souls who was blessed with wonderful parents who instilled tremendous values by living them as the example. My father, a WWII veteran, was fiercely loyal to his country and was unparalleled as a friend to many. I inherited his apparent inability to say "No" when asked to help out. His work ethic was high; he left the Navy after the war with a heart valve damaged, but worked hard physically for years until his untimely death at 49 years of age. His "do the right thing" attitude and ability to convey both parental love and high accountability formed the basis of my strong sense of ethics. My mother was herself a hard worker and, like my father, was highly involved in community affairs. I believe that their collective example of community engagement encouraged my natural gravitation to a life of service. My mother had a very strong sense of personal integrity. She was the eternal optimist and saw goodness in all people, along with a resilient sense of forgiveness for human frailties. Up until her recent death at 86 years of age, she continued to serve her community, her church, and her friends with her expertise in antiquities and her sage wisdom. I am still in mourning at her passing.

As an undergrad in college, I had the privilege of living with a diverse group. Some of these men became my life-long friends, and the lessons of their growing up with varying backgrounds fed my growing interest in valuing diversity. My wedding party included an evangelical Christian, a Jew, and an African-American, and sustaining those friendships has increased my acceptance of diverse peoples.

When I was a young rookie police officer, some of my lessons came from negative mentors...behaviors by police officers who still practiced the "traditional" policing methods. As I progressed by transferring to different police agencies, I learned the value of high standards, not only in selecting those who wear the uniform, but for their behaviors and organizational expectations. When I entered graduate school, I had the privilege to study under the late Dr. Robert Trojanowicz of Michigan State University, who is often considered the father of Community Oriented Policing. While he had never worked as a cop, his stories of lessons learned from his father, the beat cop, formulated a passion in him that was contagious. His tutelage coupled with his vision and passion led to strong ideals for me as a police officer: compassion, relationship-driven policing, respect and integrity. Later in my career, two other academics have had a profound impact on me. At the FBI National Academy, Dr. William Tafoya was the police futurist who opened my eyes to the world beyond the next three to five years. In the decades since meeting him, Bill has continued to challenge my view of the world, urging me and many others to scan the environment to seek trends and identify potential futures so that we make the best decisions we can today. Finally, Dr. Herman Goldstein, *professor emeritus* at the University of Wisconsin Law School, mentored me and many other Midwest police leaders with his visionary model of police as problem solvers. His accessibility and friendship, coupled by the same passion I saw in Bob Trojanowicz, continue to serve as inspiration. Herman challenges police to be the leaders in community problem solving, to engage those most affected by the problem, and to relentlessly analyze and pursue sustainable solutions. Long since past retirement age, his continued motto of "fire in the belly" is inspirational and has taught me to pursue my beliefs unwaveringly and with passion.

When I was first appointed as a police chief, at age 29 in my native state of Michigan, I had several veteran and wise police leaders mentor me, such as the late William Corbett, formerly of the Detroit Police and former chief of Ann Arbor and Port Huron, Michigan. From them I learned about "paying forward." They had no responsibility or obligation to assist or guide me, yet understood their critical role as teachers for the evolving generation of leaders. I benefited by watching and learning how to maintain composure and class when facing challenges, crises, and the many critical elements of a career in policing. Nationally, I was able to learn from high profile chiefs; many showed high skills, but also came with the baggage of large egos and arrogance that can accompany success. Role models like Darrell Stephens—who has served as a chief in Virginia, Florida and North Carolina as well as led national membership organizations such as PERF and Major Cities Chiefs—served as a great prototype of being intellectual, stable, humble, and courageous with his leadership style of transparency and self-accountability. I learned intellectually from several very bright leaders, but also noticed that some of them could never "connect" with their employees, and never garnered the support of the men and women who served under them. This was an important lesson. In my later years as a leader, even as I pursued academic knowledge, I worked hard to ensure I was connecting and communicating effectively with the men and women I worked with and led.

I've embraced the concept of leader as teacher. I have myself mentored and assisted over ten individuals who served under me to become CEOs, and have every expectation that many of them will far outpace my own performance. Teaching and mentoring within the organization is analogous with parenting; I've tried to maintain consistency on the important lessons both with my children as well as those I led professionally. And, in my final position as a leader, when my tenure came to an end ahead of schedule due to a change in governance and politics, I was mindful of the lessons I would give as I exited professionally. I drew on those lessons from my prior role models to carry on with class, dignity, and keeping personal integrity intact.

My early interest in diversity led to a very deliberate increase in my involvement with varied constituencies. After years of working as a police officer and leader and seeing the sense of disenfranchisement by many minorities, I made it a priority to improve the relationship between the police and the underrepresented: minorities, the aging, youth, those with mental illness, the homeless, etc. This process involved stressing values and lessons that no one person is better than another, that humans respond to respectful treatment more than authoritative, and that having a voice provides a means to improve a relationship. This approach has been highly rewarding, and led to strong growth in understanding and engagement of previously underrepresented persons with the police.

I believe that all things are driven by relationships: business, problem solving, financial transactions, communication, and our personal lives. Learning this and studying the keys to successful relationships only can yield success. Some of these keys include respect, communication skills (including listening), honesty and transparency, trust and accountability.

Adversity is an opportunity for us to practice all that we have learned. Successful people embrace adversity (some even seek it out!) as the opportunity that it is. Unsuccessful people let adversity get them down, and some even dodge their responsibilities so as to avoid adversity. Allowing adversity to provide us with leadership opportunities requires strong self-confidence, reflection, and courage without succumbing to arrogance or egotism. Some describe this as a tightrope walk. I call it a journey.

Even as I continue my journey not knowing where it will take me next, I will sustain my belief in being a servant leader, in taking every opportunity to teach (myself and others), and the importance of living the life you espouse to others. Humility, reflection, service, compassion, integrity; these are life lessons I will endeavor to live by in my personal and professional life as a way to encourage others.

About the Author

Richard W. "Rick" Myers served a career in policing from 1977-2011. After graduating with a B.S. from Michigan State University, he served as a police officer, sheriff deputy, public safety officer, and medical examiner investigator in his native state of Michigan. He subsequently received an M.S. from Michigan State University, and has attended the FBI's National Academy (156th session), LEEDS (26th Session) and the National Executive Institute (31st Session). In 1984, he began his police chief journey, leading two agencies in Michigan, one in suburban Chicago, and nationally accredited agencies in Wisconsin and Colorado. In his final chief position (Colorado), he oversaw almost 1000 employees in the U.S.' 46th largest city, and led the agency through multi-million dollar budget cuts during the ongoing recession. Despite the fiscal crisis, the agency received international accolades such as the Herman Goldstein Problem Solving Policing Award for its innovative Homeless Outreach Team and the IACP/DynCorp's Military-Civilian Collaboration Award.

Chief Myers is a Past President of the Wisconsin Chiefs of Police Association and the Society of Police Futurists International (PFI). He was on the executive board/secretary for the Police Executive Research Forum (PERF), and is presently the PERF appointee on the Commission for Accreditation of Law Enforcement Agencies (CALEA). He was recently appointed to the executive board/secretary of CALEA.

Myers has co-authored several publications of the Futures Working Group, a collaboration between the FBI and PFI. He recently co-authored a college text book, *The Future of Policing* published in 2011. He has studied international policing in Israel, Ireland, and Northern Ireland and in late 2011 was one of several U.S. police experts who traveled to Tanzania, Africa to provide training to police executives. He has been a presenter at numerous conferences and institutions on contemporary policing issues.

Richard and Cindy Myers have been married since 1979 and have proudly raised three daughters.

LEARNING, LIVING, AND LEADING

AH-HAHS:

TAKE AWAYS:

ACTION ITEM:

Honor Roll

By Enoch "Mac" McClain

As you can well imagine, with a very diverse background that includes the U.S. Marine Corps (USMC) and the Los Angeles Police Department (LAPD), I have met a number of people whom I truly admired. This became my dilemma. Which of the people on this long list would I write about? I decided to write about three men.

The first person is my stepfather, Bruce Kelly. My parents divorced when I was about eight years old. After a few years of my mother being on her own, Bruce Kelly came into our lives and married my mother. My mother, Balma, would tell me later that she had known Bruce when she was a young woman living in Mississippi. At that time, they were both married to other people. Later, his wife would die at an early age.

I can't call Bruce my stepfather; he will always be Dad to me. Dad joined the Army and would make a career of it. He would serve in a tank unit in both WWII and the Korean War. During WWII, prior to integration, Dad would be in an all Black unit that was assigned under the famous WWII General George Patton. Serving under George Patton was one of the highlights of his career. He would tell me stories of his time during WWII. Even though he was subject to the same racial discrimination as other Black military troops, not one time did I ever hear him complain or be critical of his country.

He was truly proud to have served his country. It was something he liked talking about. He would tell us of his time in Italy, Germany, and other places in faraway places. For a young kid, hearing stories of places I had only read about in books was truly exciting. It would inspire me to later volunteer to join the military.

Early on in the marriage of my mother and father, it was obvious how much they loved each other. Due to his military duty, initially, he was away most of the time. When he would come home, they were like two high school kids in love.

Dad never came home without bringing my brother and me a number of gifts. His treatment of us was great. I don't ever recall my dad or my mom telling us we had to call him "Daddy." It just evolved with us calling him that.

I really admired my dad. I never wanted to do something that would disappoint him. I remember thinking he is not a stepdad, but a dad. To this day, I don't feel comfortable using the term stepdad. It is like I'm doing a disservice to him by referring to him as my stepdad. He was a great father and deserved better. He never had kids from his first marriage and truly considered my brother and me as his sons.

When he was discharged from the service, things were the same, only he was home all the time. His skills as a father never wavered. When he died, my mother, brother, and I were devastated. A huge void now engulfed our lives.

I will always remember and love Dad. In honor of him, I would name one my daughters Kelly. My brother, Larry, would give the name Bruce as a middle name for his son, Larry.

This man was truly a man of honor.

The second person is my former commanding officer in Vietnam, Captain Jim Garrett, USMC, and a veteran of both the Korean and Vietnam wars.

I first met Captain Jim Garrett in 1966 when he was assigned as the commanding officer of my unit, Kilo Company 3rd Battalion 3rd Marine Regiment. At that time I was a Corporal squad leader, and he was a Captain who had been an enlisted Marine who converted to an officer. These unique men were called "mustangs." We weren't what you would call friends. It was more of a professional Marine relationship.

One thing that always sticks out in my mind was one day in Vietnam. We were involved in a large firefight that resulted in two Marines being wounded and a good friend of ours, Cpl. Grover Dickson, being killed. Cpl. Dickson received the Navy Cross for this battle. It is the second highest award for valor that a Marine can receive; the citation for the award was written by Captain Garrett. As usual, when something like this happens, we were all in a state of shock. As we sat on this hilltop, in the pouring rain, wondering what would come next, I looked up to see Captain Garrett standing at the top of the hill.

Forty-six years later, I can still see his face in my mind. It was a face of strength and of someone who was in complete control of his surroundings. He was like a pillar of stone. It was the face of a leader, the face of a Marine Officer, a warrior.

At that moment, with all the chaos around us, I felt a sense of calm, a feeling that with Captain Garrett in control, everything was going to be okay. I have relived that moment in time, over and over from that day forth.

At our 3/3 reunion in Washington, D.C. a few years ago, I would see Captain Garrett for the first time in over forty years. As we sat together having "a toddy," I relayed my story of him from so many years ago. He, with sadness in his eyes, said that indeed he remembered that day. It was during that discussion that our relationship went from a professional Marine relationship to that of a bond and of friendship.

During this time, we also discussed seeing an article in *Leatherneck Magazine* years ago from the mother of Cpl. Grover Dickson. In the article, she was requesting anyone who was with her son, when he died, to contact her. Although we both had seen the article, neither one of us had responded. Neither one of us had the heart to discuss the tragic death of Grover with her.

Years later, we both felt bad that we had not contacted Grover's mother and made a pact that we would do everything within our power to find her, if she was still alive. It would take over a year, but I would finally find Grover's brother and mother. I was filled with excitement when I called Captain Garrett to tell him that I had found the family. We would both speak with the family and finally had the closure we both so desperately needed.

Over the years, we would talk over the phone, sometimes over an hour; it was as if neither one of us wanted to end the conversation. We talked about our times in Vietnam, the people we met there, and our beloved Corps. Captain Garrett only met my wife, Jill, and my daughters, Kelly and Sabrina, once. Yet, somehow whenever we talked, he always remembered their names, and would ask how they were doing. He became not only a friend, but also a mentor; someone I really enjoyed being around and talking to.

In October 2010, my friend Captain Jim Garrett died. Hearing of his death was a very low point in my life. It was as if a close member of my family had died. In memory of him, I decided to fix myself a scotch, play the Marine Corps hymn, and salute a good Marine. It was at this time I would pen a letter to his wife, Rita, to express my heartfelt sorrow. Captain Garrett was a great man, Marine, and friend.

To quote Gandhi, while giving the eulogy for his friend Nehru, "…for the light that shone here was no ordinary light." He and his phone conversations will be truly missed.

He was another man of honor.

Finally, the third person is Captain Jim Docherty. I first met Captain Docherty when I was assigned as a detective to the Organized Crime and Intelligence Division. Captain Jim Docherty, or "Doc" as everyone called him, was the commanding officer of the division. Initially, I was assigned to the field following around "shady" organized crime mafia figures. After some time doing this, one of my fellow detectives and friends, Hector Zepeda, who was the adjutant for Doc, told me that Doc wanted me to come inside and work as the supervisor for the administrative section.

My first reaction was a definite no. I was enjoying my job following crooks around! Hector then proceeded to tell me, and I quote, "You don't want me to tell the Captain that you refused, do you?"

And the rest, they say, is history. The three of us became extremely close friends and became known as "the three amigos." Our friendship transcended normal friendship; it was like we were a family with the same blood.

We had an awesome responsibility of running the administration of organized crime and intelligence division. In my 30-plus years, I had the pleasure of working for a number of great captains. Jim "Doc" Docherty was not only the greatest captain on the job, but a great man.

In my position in the admin section, I got to observe his fantastic management style. I have never worked for a person who went out of his way to ensure fairness to everyone, even if it annoyed his superiors. Even when he had to take some type of negative action against a detective, he did it in a way that was professional and fair. The detective would know that Doc was only doing his job.

Doc was one of a kind. He grew up in New York and actually attended a seminary to become a priest. After making a decision to leave the seminary, he joined the New York Police Department. After a number of years on the NYPD and a tour of the Air Force during the Korean War, he came to Los Angeles and joined the LAPD.

I remember someone saying to me one day, "You and Doc are such great friends, yet you work for him. What if you screwed up and he had to take some kind of disciplinary action against you? What would you do?" My answer was quick and simple. I have so much respect for Doc that I would never do anything that would cause him to have to take action against me. You see, I would never disappoint him.

Sadly, after the three of us retired, we didn't keep close contact as we previously did. When I was told by a good friend of Doc and myself, Rita Montague, that Doc was very sick and dying, I went to see him in the hospital. As I walked into the room, he looked up from his bed with sad eyes and said, "My son has come to see me." It was all I could do to keep from crying. This man, this hero, was no longer the strong, articulate, cheerful man that I had grown to love. It was like an era in history was passing right in front of my eyes. At his funeral a week later, I had the privilege of speaking and saying goodbye to a great leader and human being.

Once again, he was another man of honor.

In closing, as I think of these three great men of honor, who were different in some ways but very alike in others, I would like to think that I have a small piece of each one of them inside of me.

My life was enhanced just knowing them. I will never forget them, and may God bless their souls. I know if there is an honor roll in heaven, these three men will be prominently on that list.

About the Author

Enoch "Mac" McClain was born in New Orleans, Louisiana on December 18, 1946. He joined the United States Marine Corps (USMC) in 1965 and served a 13-month tour in Vietnam. He was meritoriously promoted to PFC., L/Cpl., Cpl., and Sgt. His assignments included team leader, squad leader, Non Commissioned Officer in Charge (NCOIC) and primary tactics instructor for staging battalion (a unit responsible for training all Marines other than the air wing units from the rank of captain and below who were heading to Vietnam). He was also NCOIC of the base theaters in Albany, Georgia. His active duty consisted of two enlistments.

After leaving the USMC, he joined the Los Angeles Police Department (LAPD). During his thirty years in the LAPD, he accumulated more than sixty awards and commendations, including Police Officer of the Year (the Joe Sonlitner Award for leadership), and the Walter Kesterson Award. He worked numerous assignments, including vice, narcotics, metropolitan division (crime task force), SWAT, and robbery/homicide where he was partners with Detective Tom Lange from the O.J. Simpson trial. During the trial, he was tasked with interviewing some of the witnesses. He retired as a Detective III (the detective's equivalent to a first step lieutenant) and as the Watch Commander and Administrative Officer in Charge of the Organized Crime and Vice Division.

He currently is a member of the Moreno Valley Community College Community Partners. He is also the team captain and president of Semper Fi #1 Memorial Honor Detail, an all-Marine Honor Detail with 70 members. They have rendered honors for over 1700 veterans at the Riverside National Cemetery in Riverside, CA. He has been involved with the unit since 1998 and president since 2001.

He and his wife, Jill (who is Deputy Chief U.S. Pretrial Services Officer for the U.S. District Court), currently reside in Riverside, California with their two daughters, Kelly and Sabrina. He has two adult daughters by a former marriage, Deaka and Erica, a grandson, Rashad, and a granddaughter, Myla. He lives on a ranch where he cares for his horses, chickens, peacock, doves, and koi fish. His hobbies include horseback riding and boating.

HONOR ROLL

AH-HAHS:

TAKE AWAYS:

ACTION ITEM:

15-Second Windows of Fate

By Jim Fraser

Brian Willis is fond of offering challenges and opportunities that force others to grow in unique and meaningful ways. My immediate thinking, concerning Brian's challenge to select and then write my thoughts regarding those who influenced me during my lifetime, was that it was a rather simple task. That proved to be wrong. It was a far more difficult task than I had first anticipated. What I discovered is I had never given proper thought to identifying those individuals and their contributions to my personal and professional growth, style and personality. I knew who many of them were and I had some idea of their contributions, but I never actually sat down and formally cataloged those contributions and tried to put order to what would otherwise be chaos and shallow thinking. During this exercise I also came to realize there were still others who have passed through my life, and in some cases made a profound and lasting impression, but for any number of reasons I did not fully and immediately appreciate their contributions or even comprehend the impression they had made on me personally. I came to realize, in most of those cases, I would have a difficult time even identifying them by name or the circumstances of our encounter and the end product.

I came away from this experience encouraging others to formally participate in a similar activity and reap the benefits. Merely spend some quality time identifying the two or three key individuals who had the most influence on your personal development and then vigorously attempt to catalog what and how they contributed. I suggest this would prove to be a very valuable and even rewarding exercise. One of the tougher challenges was to isolate and bring the list down to just a few, as I could easily add three or four more key individuals who had a significant impact on my personal development. It became very apparent to me that I have been influenced by many and each offered something unique and useful. In the end, what these two mentors provided was usually tailored to my specific needs, personality and style and I represent their collective offerings to me.

The individual who had the most marked influence on my career in my later life was Dr. Malcolm Knowles. Malcolm is acknowledged by many as the father of the adult learning movement in the United States and I fully agree with that assessment. My encounter with Malcolm was one of those chance meetings. I have come to believe that throughout life we are presented with 15-second windows of fate, that in reality are often just unrecognized opportunities. How we respond to these "opportunities" can shape our future, although they may not seem prominent in our game plan at the time they surface and are presented to us. I call these simply "windows of fate" for they often significantly change the direction of our lives. In my case I was a U.S. Army Captain at Fort Bragg, North Carolina, and had recently completed my undergraduate degree in criminal justice and was pursuing a master's degree using the various extension courses most large military installations have available. I was at the POST Education Office talking to my educational counselor about next semester's courses. There was nothing available that semester that particularly excited me or met, to my way of thinking, my ongoing educational needs. The counselor suggested I take a course in adult learning as an elective. He said the professor was one the students had high regard for and he was a much-respected member of the education community. In fact, he is now a *professor emeritus* teaching at North Carolina State University. First of all, I had never heard of adult learning and my first inclination was it was about teaching adults—what could be so special about that? But it just meant they were older, felt a need for more education and were more likely to be motivated. In that 15-second window of fate I said, "Sure, sign me up!" I was totally unaware about the future ramifications of my decision.

Imagine my shock when this older gentleman opened his class by explaining that we were going to do what he termed "self-directed learning." We were going to work in teams and the teams were going to develop learning projects and teach those back to the class. He also said we were going to develop a journal and notebook containing our written reflections about what we had learned. Our written thoughts would be turned in at mid-term and again at the completion of the course and would represent 60% of our grade. We would also be required to negotiate a learning contract in a specified format. The learning contract would be a personal contract between professor and student and would reflect what I intended to learn and how I would learn it. We were required to write objectives, develop strategies and resources for those objectives and to indicate how and by what methods we could provide evidence we had met the objectives. Finally, we had to develop a process to have our learning validated by someone we could justify as being an expert. The learning contract was a completely new process to me and I was unsure of myself at that point. It was all so new and contrary to any of my past education. It was apparent the bulk of the learning process was being placed on me and it seemed to be a bit more than I was ready for. But Dr. Knowles challenged us to have an open mind and I drank the Kool-Aid.

Surprisingly, the process of learning was not the burden I expected it to be and I watched and became a passionate and actively involved participant. Dr. Knowles shared concepts and his perception of "andragogy" (adult learning) as contrasted with "pedagogy" (child learning) and how the process developed from his perspective. That was the real foundation for the graduate course and a process that I used repeatedly in my training career. I have modified many of these concepts today to meet the needs of the situation. My goal was to never lose the original meaning and context. Malcolm made me firmly understand it was about the process and it was the process that we use to get to the content. His courses were not content-driven but process-driven. He made a strong and believable case for the fact that adults are a rich resource for learning and they bring experiences and beliefs into the learning process that children cannot possess. It was these experiences that the process was designed to exploit and leverage. He later shared in our relationship that he was sorry he had been so quick to use the term "adults." He said as he became more experienced with the process, some of his initial thinking had begun to change and he now believed that this learning process as it has developed was just as appropriate for maturing individuals. In this definition he was referring to children as young as five or six years of age. A few years back I was President for a number of years of our local Montessori school. I was able to see the parallels between the Montessori concept—as espoused by Dr. Maria Montessori and used in our classrooms for elementary school children—and Malcolm Knowles' andragogy. There were surely differences but there were more similarities than differences. In my thirty plus years of being an adult educator and trainer, my personal experiences coincide with his beliefs, and those experiences support the fact that this process is suitable for audiences of varying sizes and age groups when they are applied with thoughtful consideration and a firm understanding of how the process works.

I was fortunate to have a continuing relationship with Malcolm for many years after being his student, through seminars and ongoing dialog by mail and telephone. Malcolm made it a point to keep everything simple so that anyone could do it. I recall this new process being exciting for me and I decided to capture it on overheads (this was the seventies and PowerPoint had not arrived just yet). I put a great deal of effort in putting together what I thought was a powerful and sterling overhead presentation on adult learning and the process I had learned from Dr. Knowles. I was certain I had captured the very essence of his work and I was quite proud of myself. I had taken careful notes and developed an outline of what I thought was superb material. I was ready to present my work to the master and dutifully impress him. Malcolm looked at the overheads and commented that while they were very good he was not interested in them as they made it seem as though using this process required extensive audio visual support. He said he sincerely appreciated my effort but this was meant to be about the process; a process any competent educator could use without the need for additional, outside support. This point has stuck with me and made a lasting impression. It had a "keep it simple stupid" sort of twist, although Malcolm would never offer his comments in such a manner—in fact, quite the opposite.

With Malcolm your efforts were always appreciated and respected. He constantly challenged us and was a very encouraging and thoughtful man. These qualities had such an impact on me as his student and later on in life. He always made you feel important and you knew he was passionate about adult learning and his students. But you also knew it was about the process and he preached getting to the content through the process. That has proven time and again to be true.

Later in life I fondly recall sending Malcolm an outline of a course I was developing for managers. He looked it over and sent me a personal, typewritten note, one I have kept and honestly cherish. The note simply said, "I was able to read the draft proposal for the FLETC Management Institute, and I am feeling a real high. You have done a simply magnificent job of applying the principles of andragogy to a very complex and demanding situation. The process described in the proposal and the attached forms are as perfect as I can imagine…I honestly tried to think of suggestions for improvement as I read the documents, Jim, and in a way I am disappointed that I couldn't think of any. They are just so right. Please let me know how things turn out. My very best wishes, Malcolm."

What a powerful message from the master himself! I have become a total disciple of Malcolm's work and I often go back and review his original course to ensure I have not moved away from the basics. Recall we kept very detailed journals and notebooks and this supports the need and use of a journal when attending training. It adds a reflective aspect as well as providing a legacy document. As a result of the foundation he provided me, I have worked in varying adult learning environments as a designer, developer and facilitator for over thirty years. I have observed his concepts move from being new and not well understood to becoming increasingly popular and part of the change process to make training better and ensuring what is trained has persistence. He would be extremely proud of the groundwork he laid but I would suggest he would not be surprised. He knew it worked and often said he wanted us to be his disciples and share what we learned openly and freely. This process effectively moves the student from being a passive and disinterested participant to one who is actively involved and who has a commitment to the learning process. I will always recall him saying that he was the one person in the classroom responsible for ensuring learning takes place; it was his job to do whatever it takes to make appropriate learning happen. He shaped me and made me a much more effective trainer than I ever would have been had he not touched my life during the end product of that original 15-second window of fate.

The second mentor I have never met but it proves an important point; there are ways to influence others other than in one-on-one or face-to-face situations. I have had email communications with him and have spent time talking about him with an individual who is probably his most successful mentee, but we never met face-to-face. Coach John Wooden is arguably the most successful basketball coach in history. I first became aware of Coach Wooden as an almost nonchalant coach on the sideline, holding a rolled-up program, as his teams generally destroyed their opponents. His demeanor and success piqued my interest and I became interested in knowing more about this person, how he was so successful and how his work already seemed to be done before the game began. How did he get so much out of players that others would not be able to produce and perform at their peak? One of those "anti-establishment" individuals was Bill Walton, an All-American under Coach Wooden. There are plenty of Bill Walton stories and I highly recommend you consider reading some of Wooden's books. You will surely be entertained by the relationship between the two while learning about how he handled Walton.

Coach Wooden was a three time All-American at Purdue University and in the Basketball Hall of Fame as both a player and a coach. The more I read about Coach Wooden the more I was impressed and the more I wanted to know. A very religious man, there appears to be no one who has ever heard him use any vulgar language in any circumstances. He believes in the basics—basics that are often overlooked but are required for real success. I was also interested in what he did with those new college basketball players he recruited from across the nation. What I learned surprised me and gave me some real food for thought. He began with the simplest of tasks: to teach these individuals, who represented the best-of-the-best of basketball players and who were all-stars in their own rights in their own regions, the basics. He sat them on the floor in a semi-circle and taught them how to properly put on their socks and shoes. How basic can you get? Coach Wooden's defense was that putting on your socks and shoes properly were likely never taught—as a young person you just muddled through the process. No one took the time to teach you those very basic things because they thought they were just that, too basic. The real key to why he started there was that in his judgment you could not be an All-American at UCLA with blisters on your feet. This has caused me to always think about basics and consider if my students have been properly trained in the basics to the point that they can be ultimately successful. I have come to realize that we often start at a higher level than we should and believe they possess knowledge and skills that they have not learned yet. Wooden's lessons on teaching the basics had a profound impact on me as a trainer.

During an interview Coach Wooden was asked, "Is it true that you used to instruct your players on how to put on their shoes and socks before each game or practice?" His response was pure Wooden: "Absolutely. I picked that up when I was teaching in high school. We had a lot of blisters, and I found out that a lot of the players didn't smooth out all the wrinkles around their heels and around their little toes, places where the blisters are apt to occur. Then I found out that they didn't lace their shoes properly and oftentimes they wore shoes that were a size too large. With all the quick-stop turning, changes of direction, changes of pace on a hard floor you have in basketball, this would cause blisters. So, I thought it was very important that I'd check their shoe size and how they put their socks on. I hoped they would take a few extra seconds to smooth out the wrinkles around the heel and the toes and hold the sock up while they put their shoe on. I think it was important. And I know from the time I started in high school that we greatly reduced the number of blisters that we'd have, so I continued that throughout my coaching. I know a number of players laughed about it. They probably still laugh about it now. But I stuck to it. I think to some degree it helped team unity. I believed in that and I insisted on it."

During my research on Coach Wooden I came across some of his material that was not widely published. I liked what he had to say and wanted to use it in my future training. I decided the best approach was to send him an email and explain that I liked the material, how I would use it, ask for his permission while at the same time asking him to validate what was published. I was surprised to receive an email from Coach Wooden himself. I also learned during my research that he was so inundated by mail that volunteers had formed a Team Wooden brigade to respond to his mail. In his email he asked about St. Simons Island, Georgia where I live. Coach Wooden said in his email that he was stationed with the U.S. Navy on St. Simons during World War II. (Note: FLETC, The Federal Law Enforcement Training Center, is on the former Glynco Naval Air Station and our area is dotted with airfields that were used for aviator training during WWII. One of the auxiliary fields was on St. Simons Island about fifteen miles from FLETC.) He recalled that during one hurricane evacuation they had gone from their splinter village to the King and Prince Hotel, a more secure facility on our island. I responded back to him and sent him pictures of the current hotel. That was the start of our personal email communications.

The article and the concept he presented in it were about how he trained and his personal laws of learning. It was apparent he always considered himself a teacher first and foremost and that was his primary orientation. In the article he discussed that he believed the best approach with his players was short, focused drills of five- to eight-minute duration (none more than ten minutes in length) rather than scrimmages, which the players preferred. Even when he scrimmaged, those who were not participating were required to shoot free throws. Everyone was doing something and there was no time to simply stand around and watch. To get into the preferred scrimmage a player had to make ten free throws in a row. When they did that they replaced a scrimmager and he had to do the same if he wanted back on the floor. In this article his emphasis was on the drills and their importance and why he was concerned about the player's attention span during their training. In the article he also discussed what he loosely referred to as Wooden's Laws of Learning. First he would explain and then he would demonstrate and then he would ask the players to imitate what was demonstrated during which time he would critique their performance. These were the first three of eight laws of learning. The other five were Repetition, Repetition, Repetition, Repetition and Repetition. He reinforced the need and importance of repetition in skill development. However, he used different drills to teach the same material. He wanted his players to see it from a different perspective and the repetition didn't have to occur in the same session. His objective was for them to repeat the model over and over, a bit each day until the skill became automatic. His approach was clear and to use his words, "You can't cram it all into them at once."

A few years ago I was traveling west for a training session and had a stopover in San Antonio. In a chance encounter in the airport I had the opportunity (another one of these 15 seconds of fate opportunities BTW) to end up sitting next to Bill Walton, at the time an NBA Basketball analyst and arguably one of Coach Wooden's most successful disciples. This giant of a man sat down in the seat next to me during what turned out to be an extended weather delay. We were in the common area between adjoining gates as he was traveling in the opposite direction. We engaged in a conversation about the weather and TSA (at that time they were doing additional security at the individual gates and were a somewhat new agency) and we laughed about their procedures and how and why they were and were not selecting individuals for extra scrutiny. When they selected an elderly and apparent grandmother type, we both had something to say and it wasn't very complimentary of their professionalism. Because we had introduced ourselves upon first sitting down, I felt obliged later in our discussions to ask him about Coach Wooden and he was very willing to share some fascinating stories about the coach. He told me that not only was the story about the shoes and socks true but that he has taken his sons to Wooden's house and had him do the same training with them. He said spending time, any time, with Coach Wooden was always a treat and there was more being learned than just putting on socks and shoes. It was obvious that Bill Walton had a great respect and love for Coach Wooden that came through loud and clear during the few hours we spent together waiting for the weather to clear. Our conversation served to validate the qualities of Coach Wooden and his ability to lead others.

Coach Wooden has had a marked influence on how I train and how I now think as an individual. What I learned from him made me carefully review how I was doing business as a trainer. Were my sessions too long? Was I trying to cram too much into them at one time? Was I soliciting feedback to see if they were getting it? The bottom line is it has changed my ways of doing business and there are two important, learned behaviors here. First is the basics—never forget the basics. Ensure they know and can do what they must be able to do to be successful. It is easy to jump over the basics or assume they know things they may not know or be able to do. We assume far too much sometimes. The second important lesson was repetition. Students are not always fond of repetition but we can find ways to make it happen in such a way that it is fun or not obviously repetitive. Repetition can be extended over a period of time, reinforcing material day after day, but in creative and meaningful ways. These are the challenges we face as trainers. Teachers like Coach John Wooden are role models for us and we need to learn about the processes they follow and why and then follow in their footsteps. They are, in my estimation, the correct role models to emulate. I am happy I took the time to learn about the man and the reasons for his successes.

About the Author

Jim is a retired U.S. Army Colonel and is the Principal in Fraser and Associates, Inc. located in St. Simons Island, GA. His experiences and activities include training development; advanced instructor training, supervisor, management, and executive training; adult learning; presentation procedures; special events planning and training; emergency and critical incident management; antiterrorism, security and contingency planning; and crisis management. He specializes in the training of law enforcement personnel in these various disciplines. He was the contract developer for and facilitated the CA POST Master Instructor Development Training Program and Advanced Instructor Training through 2011; both programs are adult learning/experience-based instructor development programs and are integral parts of POST's tiered Instructor Development Institute. In 1999 he was selected as an Excellence in Instruction awardee. He is the 2001 Robert Presley Institute of Criminal Investigation Founder's Award recipient and was honored as the 2009 POST "Bud" Hawkins award recipient, POST's most prestigious training award.

15-Second Windows of Fate

Ah-Hahs:

Take Aways:

Action Item:

I Get by with a Little Help from a Friend

By Tom Cline

Asked to write this piece by good friend, Ron Scheidt, I accepted the challenge and soon regretted it, procrastinating until the last. It meant reliving many of the poor choices I've made. I didn't think of my life-long good.

As a child I wasn't very good at sports and ignored by my father who had more interest in work and beer, things not conducive to family life. I will give him this though: he treated my mom well and brought home the check. My mother did most of the parenting. Thankfully she was moral and had a firm hand. But moms can go only so far with boys; they need men around to learn how to act like one. Boy Scout leaders and parish priests provided role models through grammar school; however, in high school I fell through the cracks and found no mentor in the system.

Before joining the Chicago Police Department in the late sixties, I had floundered for several years, abandoned my faith and bought the philosophy of sex, drugs and rock and roll. The cops I met were not guardians and selfless individuals portrayed in the TV shows of the fifties and sixties. One old cop told me, "Kid, dis is the best job in da world. Ya kin come ta work tired, broke, horny an' hungry an' go home after eight wit all doze needs satisfied."

Yes, there were compassionate cops and aggressive ones who loved locking up bad guys, but most of them engaged in behaviors that are unacceptable today.

Burned out by the mid-seventies, I took two leaves of absence to learn Spanish and took up outdoor adventure to escape. In 1980, a new sergeant who was assigned to neighborhood relations persuaded me to go to work for him as a community services officer. He was a mentor, old school, tough and selfish, but interested in doing good things in the community. He saw talent that I did not and used me to organize a police athletic league and community events, to scrounge resources from local business, and to entertain at functions. Life got better and my cynicism diminished. I was put in charge of a Police Explorer unit, and realized I was a role model for these teens. I started changing my poor behavior.

I married in 1982 and we had our first child in 1984. In a moment of saving grace, watching my son mimic me, I realized that if I continued to be the person I was I'd have a jerk on my hands in fifteen years. It was time to change. I returned to church and surrounded myself with people that were better than me. I studied the Catholic faith, and the more I studied the more it made sense. Doors opened, I entered. On becoming involved with a group of conservative Catholic men, I met an older Irish fellow, a Korean War vet, who was an English teacher from one of Chicago's toughest ghetto schools and a political activist who had raised four children and was still in love with his wife. He had the patience of a saint, wisdom and understanding beyond anyone I'd ever met.

I think he initially felt sorry for me and we started meeting regularly, most often to attend Mass or spiritual formation. This routine continues even today. After our meetings we break bread and talk. He asks questions about how I am caring for my wife and kids. "When was the last time you took her out? I can babysit." I tell him my worries and concerns, and he always has a story from literature or the Bible that offers reliable options. After checking on my family's status, he moves on to my work and often brings me news stories and research about leadership, ethics and law enforcement, insisting always that I am doing more good than I know. I suspect he has more influence on the Chicago Police Department and law enforcement than he knows.

His name is John McCartney, a distant cousin of the Beatle, Paul. A better role model I could not have. Retired now, when not mentoring me or several others, he writes letters to national and local newspapers and edits everything I write with honesty. Further, he hands out pro-life literature to teens outside Chicago area high schools. This has almost gotten him locked up on more than one occasion by complaining principals and teachers who find freedom of speech offensive. He stands his ground and tactfully explains the law to responding officers.

John has become a father figure for me, nurturing the good in me and helping suppress the bad. He regularly helps calibrate my moral compass by encouraging and giving hope when I'm discouraged.

Not only has John mentored me, but also my wife and children, who respect him and have sought his counsel. To many, his views may seem antiquated. Not to me. He sees things from a supernatural point of view, always ready to give another the benefit of the doubt, keeping in mind that humans are flawed and justice and mercy must be appropriately mixed. His vision is clearer than most in today's culture where so much seems upside down and illogical.

They say that the right mentor appears when you are ready. Perhaps that is true. I do not know why I've been worthy to strike this mentor and friendship with such a good person, but I do recognize that with this comes the responsibility to help others. For that I am thankful. It is my redemption.

About the Author

Tom Cline is President of the International Association of Ethics Trainers. He and his wife, Sandi, publish *Integrity Talk Journal*, serving ethics trainers striving to make a difference. Tom earned a MBA and MAP, trains for the Chicago Police Department and others through the USA.

Cop Tales! Vol. 1 (Never Spit in a Man's Face...Unless His Mustache is on Fire)

Surviving Storms – Non-Tactical Career Survival for Law Enforcers

Contact Tom at Iaethicstrainers@comcast.net

I Get by with a Little Help from a Friend

Ah-Hahs:

Take Aways:

Action Item:

Model Your Role Models, Heroes, and Mentors

By Randy Zales

Role models exemplify behaviors that we not only admire but idolize. Our heroes inspire us to conquer our enemies and overcome our challenges: we wish we could be like them, if only for a day. We also seek out mentors who are highly accomplished in skills that we admire. As it turns out, however, role models, heroes, and mentors are imperfect, just like us. They go through tough times and awkward moments; they have slumps and flaws. That is why I believe it is better to emulate the admirable and inspiring strategies of our role models, heroes, and mentors rather than modeling after the models themselves.

Growing up as a kid in the 1980s, superheroes like Batman, Superman, and Captain America were infallible. We idolized them for their power, their superior skills when faced with danger, and their commitment to doing what was right. When contrasted with today's not-so-perfect portrait of many superheroes, like the Watchmen, these heroes seem to be lacking in some element of moral character. They possess the same superior power and they defeat the bad guys when it comes down to it, but they are also narcissistic, selfish, and don't always play well with others; the ends justify the means. Some of their strategies, behaviors, and attitudes are worthy of our emulation—others are not.

Many of us know about great leaders who are or were terrible fathers or husbands. We hear about famous businessmen who start business empires on the back of a napkin but ultimately lose it through excess or lack of judgment. We learn about the world-class officer, operator, or soldier whose real-life exploits and skills are the stuff of legends but whose life off the job is consumed by serious personal problems. These examples just scratch the surface of why and how people are disappointed when their role models ultimately do not live up to the expectations of their admirers. Let me first share a personal example as to why I believe it's better to model the strategies of my role models, heroes, and mentors instead of the heroes themselves.

As a young lieutenant in the Army in the 1990s, one of my heroes and role models was the legendary Colonel Charlie Beckwith, a charismatic and controversial Army colonel who risked his career by fighting for a more flexible special operations unit. Col. Beckwith eventually founded the First Special Forces Operational Detachment Delta, better known as Delta Force. I was inspired by his dedication to accomplishing the mission, taking care of his men, and providing realistic training. I understood his actions as a statement against the status quo, especially the status quo that allowed officers to make decisions that furthered their careers instead of prioritizing what was best for the mission or the men. I admired him not only for his willingness to stand up to superiors and rock the boat over important issues but also for his operational prowess and care for his men. I wanted to be the kind of officer that he was. When I shared this role model with an assigned officer mentor during my basic officer course he told me, "If you copy him in today's Army, your men will probably love you, but you are going to have some real challenges with your superiors and will never make it to Major." I modeled Col. Beckwith anyway. Why not? He and his men achieved the mission no matter what the circumstances. His men loved him, and together they hammered whatever got in their way.

When all you have is a hammer, every obstacle is a nail

As it turned out, the assigned mentor was not completely wrong, although modeling my hero's "mission first, men always" attitude worked extremely well. This assessment is not based on my opinion or belief: it's based on the fact that in the military you either achieve the mission or you don't. My troops achieved the mission time and time again. While at the 1-505 PIR, we had the highest passing rate on the expert field medical badge in the history of the 82nd Airborne Division up to that point. We excelled at operational readiness inspections and at our platoon's evaluation on real-world deployments and we exceeded standards at the

Army's Joint Readiness Training Center. At every opportunity, my NCOs and I created an environment of taking care of our men both personally and professionally. Sometimes this took the form of specialized training; sometimes it meant loaning some cash in between paydays; other times it meant taking the time to help them through personal problems so they could get their focus back on the mission. We respected and cared for each other, and when it was time to work they shared my passion for mission accomplishment. I never thought of myself as a good leader and I made a lot of mistakes, but by focusing on what I modeled from my extended mentors I developed a reputation for getting the mission done and taking care of my men. If I had stopped at this point—modeling the "mission first, men always" strategy but not the other aspects of my hero—I would have been much better off. However, in addition to adopting Beckwith's mantra, I also argued with superior officers, rocked the boat, and hammered anyone who got in the way of completing the mission or who interfered with my men. I jumped at conflict instead of seeking cooperation. In hindsight many of the conflicts with peers and superiors could have been avoided or mitigated if I would have modeled a few of the strategies instead of the entire person. In the years to come, I learned strategies from other role models and experts that allowed me to become more persuasive and tactful; a better communicator. More importantly, I learned a modeling process that I have used both personally and professionally to this very day.

Modeling these Strategies is a Process

Modeling is a process that people use to analyze and identify crucial patterns of strategies, behaviors, and attitudes that are at the root of success for outstanding individuals, teams, and companies. These patterns can be codified, learned, and repeated to increase your chances of similar success. Let me give you a real-world example. In the early 1980s, the U.S. Army experimented with a new training initiative called the Jedi Project. One aspect of this program was about experimenting with the modeling technique to increase the efficiency of .45 pistol shooting training. One of the major reasons this skill was chosen was because the .45 had a reputation for being hard to handle: some shooters could get no reproducible results with the weapon, while others swore by its effectiveness. Here's how the task force used the modeling skill. First, they identified the three best .45 shooters. Second, these experts were questioned in detail about their beliefs surrounding shooting. They were asked about their confidence levels, what shooting meant to them, what pre-shooting rituals they engaged in, and what they said to themselves while shooting. Third, the experts were observed while shooting: stance, body posture, muscle tone, pistol grip, arm position, and breathing. Finally, the task force distilled all the information gathered and extracted the one critical element that all three experts had in common: mental rehearsal. This element is known as the "difference that makes the difference," the element that, if taken away, drastically reduces the rate of success. This element may be a belief, a physical action, or a mental exercise. For these expert shooters, mentally rehearsing the visual, auditory, and kinesthetic details of shooting—the sights, sounds, and feelings—was this key element.

After eliciting all of these physical and mental elements of the experts' strategies, the task force trained their test group by using the specific physical components and mental attitudes in the exact order they had modeled from the experts. In order to remove any bias, a control group of shooters was trained in the conventional manner. The result? According to Colonel John B. Alexander (USA Retired) in his book *The Warriors Edge* the control group, which received the conventional training, had 73% of the shooters qualified after 27 hours of training. In the test group, the ones modeling the experts, 100% of the shooters qualified after only 12 hours of training: a compelling result. This study led me to my first role model on the process of modeling.

The key man behind the Army's modeling project was none other than bestselling author Anthony Robbins. Anthony and I worked together in business for a decade after my military service, applying modeling concepts to help improve individual and organizational performance. This time, however, I did not get caught up in the entire personality of my role model; I had learned to model the strategies instead of the person.

How to Discover and Model the Strategies

Modeling involves observing and mapping the successful processes that lie beneath an exceptional performance. It is the process of taking complex actions, or even a series of actions, and breaking them into chunks that are small enough to be individually analyzed. The purpose of modeling is to create a practical map, or "model," of that strategy. This model can then be used to reproduce or simulate some aspect of that performance by anyone who is motivated to do so.

Step one: Identify a role model

If you don't have a specific role model in mind, look for someone who is already accomplishing the result you're looking to achieve. Another approach is to find a number of people who are experts at this skill; you can refine the strategy even more quickly by comparing their actions in later steps. Keep any actions that are either repeated immediately by multiple experts or stand out as important to you. Actions that are part of only one person's strategy need to be tested to determine whether they are unnecessary to the overall strategy and should be eliminated or if they are necessary and should be retained.

Step two: Put the role model in the role

In order to accurately draw out the specific results strategy, the expert must be performing the strategy that you are modeling. If you are merely having a conversation about the strategy rather than engaging in the strategy itself, the model must become "fully associated" with the experience as if he is really performing it. One simple way to get a person fully associated is by asking him to remember a specific time when he was actually achieving the result and to step back into that experience as if it were currently happening. Some people can better imagine the experience with their eyes closed. Remember, many experts have become so proficient in their skill that they unconsciously follow their success strategy. If you attempt to elicit the strategy when it is not actually being performed or the expert isn't fully associated with it, you may get intellectual responses that do not accurately reflect all the details of the strategy. He honestly may not know or be able to describe exactly what he does, but you can figure it out by following these steps.

Step three: Uncover the expert's focus

Think like an interrogator or an investigator. While your role model is performing or fully associated, ask him specific, detailed questions about his beliefs and attitudes surrounding the particular skill. What are you focusing on at this step or point? What emotion are you feeling at this step? Any question that helps your role model share his focus or beliefs is a great question. Asking "What else?" after the answers, prompts the expert to think even more intensely about the performance, and very often produces valuable responses. Another useful technique is to ask the same question in different ways and compare the answers. Are they consistent?

Step four: Elicit the specific results strategy

While your role model is performing or fully associated, ask him questions to determine the specific sequence of actions that he takes. Ask, "What is the very first thing that you see, hear, feel or do when you are doing X?" Then ask, "What is the next thing that you see, hear, feel or do when you are doing X?" Continue asking until the sequence is complete. If during this process your role model stops performing or becomes too academic—answering your questions instead of experiencing the answers—stop and have him get back in role before continuing.

In this step you are looking for the specific ingredients, the amount of each ingredient, and the exact order that each ingredient is added so that when you finish you have a complete recipe. For example, in modeling the .45 pistol shooting experts, the three experts all revealed that prior to each shooting match they mentally rehearsed every shot. By specifically including the visual, auditory, and kinesthetic modes in these questions you prompt your expert to convey all the details they have stored in their subconscious mind. You want to know what they picture, what they say to themselves, what they feel and do, and when during the sequence each of these things happen. This is your recipe.

Make sure that your role model's answers and your observations also include his specific physiology (posture, gestures, breathing, facial expressions, etc.) at each step. Tailor your questions and observations to draw out as much detailed information as you possibly can. This will allow you to pick up on the fine distinctions that even your role model may not be aware of!

Step five: Find the "difference that makes the difference"

If you were able to model more than one person, compare the answers you received. Is there any one component that all experts agreed was essential? Compare your new recipe with the strategy of someone who is getting good, but not outstanding, results. What is/are the main difference(s)? Finally, ask your expert! In his opinion, what is the most important element in his strategy? Now that you have your expert's strategy for success, you can start to follow the recipe.

As you go along, you'll add your own style to these five steps and even make improvements based on what is important to you. More importantly, be unique and be yourself. Admiring, respecting, and even emulating another person's skills, habits, or results does not mean that you have to be a clone or live up to their achievements. In this case, you may want to model Bruce Lee's perspective: "I'm not in this world to live up to your expectations and you're not in this world to live up to mine." As for me, I continue to focus on my mission and my men.

About the Author

Randy Zales is a recognized authority on leadership, performance improvement and developing train-the-trainer programs. He works engagements in the US and abroad for Fortune 500 companies, franchise organizations, private companies, start-ups and law enforcement agencies including the Department of Homeland Security and the Federal Law Enforcement Training Center (FLETC). Randy is a former Paratrooper and US Army officer who served in command and operational assignments with rapid deployment units. Randy has a BA from Michigan State University and earned his Master's Degree from Central Michigan University.

MODEL YOUR ROLE MODELS, HEROES, AND MENTORS

AH-HAHS:

TAKE AWAYS:

ACTION ITEM:

What have you learned about yourself as a result of reading this book?

Tom's Legacy

By Randy Sutton

In 1896, Alfred Nobel, the inventor of dynamite, would leave a legacy known throughout the world. He would use his vast fortune to create something that would come to symbolize and celebrate the greatest scientific and social achievements of man in the twentieth century and beyond. Today the Nobel Peace Prize is considered one of history's greatest achievements and the idea behind its development has lived on through many generations. Without a doubt, the financial rewards to the recipients of Mr. Nobel's grand plan act as a fuel to further the idea that brought about its birth. But his true legacy was not his tremendous wealth. His true legacy was the ideals that he believed in so strongly: His belief that man should be celebrated for his contributions to his fellow man. That was the true legacy of Alfred Nobel.

Many years ago, I was left a legacy by a man whose ideals would come to touch the lives of many people that he would never know or even meet. I was a young police officer who believed more in the strength of my badge than in the heart that beat behind it. My world consisted of two distinct colors at that point, and they were shaded only by statutes and ordinances. I led the department in arrests and am probably still remembered for issuing a speeding ticket to a Nun who believed that "sanctuary" applied when driving onto the property of the convent with me in pursuit. I was only too happy to prove otherwise. I worked tirelessly in my solo attempt to stamp out crime and transgression and truly believed in my strategy of "zero tolerance."

Police departments like any other workplace have a supervisory hierarchy that is guided by fate. By the luck of the draw you can be assigned to a Sergeant or a boss that is competent or not, self-serving or nurturing, principled or unscrupulous. I was fortunate, as my Sergeant was not only highly respected but also respectful of others. I had seen him in action many times and truly admired his steely courage and his quiet humor. I looked to him for guidance during the bloom of my young police career and he did little to disappoint me. But there was one conversation above all others that 25 years later still reverberates through my memories like the tolling of a bell. We were having breakfast one chilly autumn morning, looking out of the greasy windows of an all-night diner as a fiery dawn broke. The discussion was fairly one-sided with me recounting the long night's events, including a domestic dispute with a particularly argumentative husband whom I had gleefully handcuffed and jailed. When I was done bragging about my exploits, Tom said nothing for a moment. He simply looked at me over the streaked white porcelain coffee mug he held between his two hands and I knew by his silence that his thoughts were dancing. He placed the mug into the coffee-ringed saucer with a gentle clatter and said, "Randy, you're a good cop. You have all of the instincts necessary to sniff out bad guys, an excellent working knowledge of the law and admirable dedication." I basked in the remarks but felt uneasy about what else might be coming.

"But let me ask you one question." *Uh oh*, I thought. "Can you tell me the difference between being a good cop…and a great cop?" I must have stammered something but to this day I cannot remember what. I do remember his eyes crinkling with amusement at my response, and then with the earnest expression that I came to know well in the years to come he said, "The difference between being a 'good cop' and a 'great cop' is…compassion." There are moments in your life that have special significance. Moments that create clarity in thought and perspective and for me, that conversation is often revisited. The concept of compassion has come to define my view of not only my profession but also how I conduct my life. Most importantly though, it is that message that I have passed on to many a young and eager cop in whose future I am proud to have played a role. It is this rich legacy of thought that was fortunately bequeathed to me by a man who has proven again and again to be a mentor, friend and true hero.

I eventually left that police department for several reasons but the most significant being that I felt that the leadership of the agency utilized fear, intimidation and power as their personal choice of leadership techniques. This led to poor morale amongst the employees that manifested itself as fragmented loyalties, promotions based on nepotism and personnel turnover. This continued for several more years after I left until the then Chief retired, and a metamorphosis took place. The new Chief brought with him an entirely different philosophy of leadership. He created an environment of unity by listening to the needs of his officers. Changes were made to how shift schedules were developed, promotions and assignments were based, and how discipline was meted out. However, the most significant change was that the employees came to believe that their leadership cared about the law enforcement mission as well as about them. Recruitment and retention improved, officers distinguished themselves and were recognized for their achievements, and a culture of pride became evident. Who was the man that ushered in this amazing change? You guessed it, the same man whose words and guidance had touched me those many years ago. Once again his philosophy would trickle down through the men and women of the organization that would affect a new generation of young cops.

The decades have flown swiftly and just the other day, I sat at my kitchen table, a mug of steaming coffee before me as I looked at the two photographs displayed in the "shadowbox" commemorating my retirement from policing after 34 years. On one side was a black and white photo of my "rookie" days and on the other was a professional color portrait complete with braid and gold bars. My thoughts rushed back through the years, and the moments that defined my career flashed along in a parade of joy, sadness, satisfaction and pride. In the reflection of the glass that covered a box of memories I caught a glimpse of two men in a diner where one word changed one of them forever.

About the Author

Randy Sutton was a Police Officer for ten years in New Jersey and recently retired as a Lieutenant with the Las Vegas Metropolitan Police Dept. He is the Author of *TRUE BLUE Police Stories by Those Who Have Lived Them* and *A COP'S LIFE* and *TRUE BLUE To Protect and Serve*. He is a nationally known speaker on the subject of Law Enforcement Ethics and Leadership and is the Founder of www.celebtratinglegacy.com, a website devoted to helping people live better lives by honoring themselves, their families and their memories. Randy can be contacted at randy@celebratinglegacy.com.

Tom's Legacy

Ah-Hahs:

Take Aways:

Action Item:

Acknowledgements — Brian Willis

This project would have been impossible without the love, support, guidance and patience of my family. My wife, Lynda, and I have been married since June 6, 1981. Her unconditional love and support for me, regardless of the hours I work or the time I spend on the road speaking and around North America, continually amazes me. As I work through this project, I realize I am not always being the husband she needs and deserves, but she loves and supports me anyway. Lynda's selfless attitude and willingness to help others is a continual source of inspiration.

My two sons, Jesse and Cody, are a constant source of pride, motivation and inspiration to me. Their maturity, their creativity, their willingness to pursue their dreams; their love, their support and their wise counsel are priceless to me and a constant reminder that I must always work to be the father they need and deserve me to be. Cody used his photography and artistic skills to create an amazing cover for the book, and Jesse used his creativity to write a powerful submission for the book. I sought their feedback and counsel throughout this project on a variety of issues. They now serve as mentors and role models for me.

My parents, Bob and Terry Willis, are my heroes, my role models, and my mentors. I have not always demonstrated my love and respect for the sacrifices they made for me, and I have not always been the son they deserved me to be and needed me to be. For that I am truly sorry. They have, however, always been there to love me unconditionally and to support me. For that I am truly grateful.

My brothers, Jim and Larry, and my sister Sandy also serve as role models and mentors for me through how they live their lives as sons and daughter, as brothers and sister, as husbands and wife, as mother and father, as friends, as teachers, and as community members. It is their laughter and their commitment to family; their love for each other, of their spouses and children; and their love of life that serves to inspire me. I am truly blessed to have such a supportive, fun and loving family.

I would like to thank Ron Scheidt for lighting the fire of this project with his article *Am I That Man?*, originally written for the book, *If I Knew Then: Warrior Reflections*. That article and his question, "Is there a book in this question?" was the catalyst for this project. Ron's friendship and support have meant a great deal to me over the years.

Of course this book would not have been possible without the support of the many people who made time in their very busy lives to write their essays and share their stories. Each one of them leads extremely busy lives and has huge demands on their time. Despite those demands they carved out time from their schedules to write for this book. They asked nothing in return; they simply wanted to do their part in helping men become better sons, brothers, husbands, fathers, leaders, role models and mentors. They endured my countless e-mails asking for updates and asking for favors. Without them there would be no book. They will never know how many lives they have influenced through their story and they are ok with that. They did not do it for the glory; they did not do it for money. They did it because they believed it was the right thing to do. Ron and I can never truly express our appreciation for the contribution these men made to this book and the contribution they make to the world on a daily basis.

I want to thank Bob Delaney for his commitment to excellence as a New Jersey State Trooper, an NBA referee and now as an author and speaker. Through his work with law enforcement and military personnel dealing with the effects of post-traumatic stress Bob has changed lives and saved lives with his message of hope. Despite his extremely demanding schedule Bob was gracious enough to honor our request to write the Foreword for this book and for that both Ron and I are extremely grateful.

There have been so many people outside of my family who have served as role models, mentors and heroes for me in my life. I worry that if I try to list them all here I will leave someone out, but I need to say thank you. The people I worked with in the Calgary Police Service Skills and Procedures Unit had a profound effect on me personally and professionally and their friendship continues to impact my life in positive ways. Mike Starchuk, Wally Muller, Chris Butler and Darren Leggatt continue to counsel me and mentor me and for that I am grateful.

My association with ILEETA (International Law Enforcement Educators and Trainers Association) has had a huge impact in my personal and professional growth and development. Ed Nowicki and Harvey Hedden took a chance on me by asking me to be part of the Advisory Board and have continued to help, guide, and mentor me. Their support and friendship has meant a great deal to me. The friendships I have developed though ILEETA are too many to mention and have had a huge influence in my life. There are a few, however, who I must acknowledge as their friendship, support and influence over the last ten years has been invaluable. Thank you to Mark 'Sponge' Zbojniewicz, Randy Meyers, Tim Janowick, John Bostain, Chuck Soltys, Marcus Young, and Chuck Remsberg. You continue to support me, inspire me, challenge me to learn and to think differently. To all the 'Below 100' family, thank you for saving lives.

In the production of every book there is always a great deal of work that goes on behind the scenes. I would like to thank Vivian Moser for her editing skills. Vivian played an important role in the final product of this book. Diana Ennen, Theresa Scholes and Yvonne McCoy from BizEase helped immensely in taking the book from the manuscript phase to a real book. Their expertise in all phases of project management, marketing and typesetting is greatly appreciated.

Acknowledgements—Ron Scheidt

This book is an amalgamation of ideas, talents, sacrifices, contributions, and encouragement by many and varied individuals.

Professionally I would like to thank Brian Willis, my visionary partner in this project, for his tutelage and unrelenting pursuit of excellence. I would also like to acknowledge the contributing authors who, without hesitation, gave so freely their time and talents. These men have unselfishly given us access into their private lives and thoughts that both celebrate their strengths and expose their weaknesses. Their stories inspire, encourage, challenge, and entertain.

Personally I would like to thank my sons, Evan and Martin, for all of the love, rewards and challenges of fatherhood. Furthermore I would like to thank Evan, the journalist, for helping convert my vision into words. I want to acknowledge my nephews, Mike and Tim, who lost a father when I lost my brother. I see so much of their dad in them and there is no greater compliment. I am thankful to my mom, Fran, who was my biggest cheerleader. I miss her every day. I also want to thank my wife, Jeri, who is my best friend and my soul mate. She has been a constant source of love and support and she inspires me to want to be a better man.

Though attempted through this project, words are truly insufficient to describe the gratitude and love I have for my brother, Bud, and my coach, Bill. They ARE that man.

CPSIA information can be obtained at www.ICGtesting.com
Printed in the USA
BVOW011614140213

313286BV00001B/1/P